Abundance

NOW!!!

For all mankind! Set yourself free. A 21st Century African approach to past-scarcity

By Vincent Happy Mnisi MSc, Esq

foreword by Ras Lawrence Davis

"*This world needs love!*"

"*The goal of the future is full unemployment, so we can all be creative! That's why we all need to destroy this present Capitalistic-Political-Economical-Social-System*".....

Foreword by Ras Lawrence Davis from New York City.

"In this time as the world stands still. Yet as men we have to think forward. We have to imagine what is possible. All through the passage of time a certain Man would dream of something else and we as humanity should give that some Consideration, the current life can't be the all. He who would glimpse that there is enough for all. that the Planet produces Abundance. That Man will start the scratching of the walls of limitation, He will begin the digging of the hole in that wall, for the escape from limitation and, that hole will eventually allow the whole wall to tumble. Vincent Happy Mnisi is that man at this time. An Abundant Life is what this book gives, rising as a tool for that result. 2020 is an opportunity to recalibrate the situation of the World and its relationship with the Black People and the Black Man Himself redefining Himself into his own destiny. When you think of the People on the planet and their movement, you see limits set by others. All you see routines. The doldrums of one's life. That is, to wake up, go to work, back home and to go to church of sorts and a movie at it's best. Then add the few interactions that come between. We, with this book, Abundance Now!!!, are allowing One's mind to glimpse new pathways and an alternative life and it's possibilities. Let us not fall back to the routines that are normal. Stretch Yourself and join forces with those who are awake or becoming awake. Time to re-define Ourselves a place in the Sun."

By Ras Lawrence Davis. a speck

Contents

"Once poverty is gone, we'll need to build museums to display its horrors to future generations. They'll wonder why poverty continued so long in human society and how a few people could live in luxury while billions dwelt in misery, deprivation and despair."...By Muhammad Yunus,

Introduction

In a Post-Scarcity article written by Captain Capitalism (2020) he stated "Imagine a World where we can all grow your own food in an entirely automated greenhouse or on land issued out to everybody on Earth. As normal our water falls readily from the sky or wells up from the earth from boreholes and can be filtered and cleaned immediately. Everyone has access to abundant free energy from the sunlight and when one desires an electronic device or a motored product, you can get a design online and are able customise it immensely, and fabricate it locally or have it delivered using an efficient automated delivery service. And your children and you will have access to the best education online ever conceived, for free. What need will humanity have to engage with a monetary system?"

The best way we can all contribute to a Post-Scarcity World Economy (PSWE) is by sharing the generally-privately owned natural resources to all Humanity. Governments must start by nationalising all natural resources which will be a New Dawn and that humanity must learn how to cultivate their own food. Governments should issue out land, seeds and then show people the exact techniques of growing it for free on the Internet. Everyone gets to contribute to the open-source world society including educational materials allowing people to study whatever you're passionate about and ponder how you can benefit and add purpose to Humanity. Everyone perceives that social transformation appears or get's decreed from the hall's of legislators' in halls of leadership but history has proved it has constantly grown from the bottom up, from the young vibrant intelligent minds who appreciate and think distinctly different and express what's on their minds, Revolution's were always built from the youth "THE YOUTH ARE THE FUTURE". The internet is the hub of knowledge readily accessible to all Humanity, it's time Society began utilising it to effectively in their lives and also benefit from it too. It is all about information, and more information-management is now the key determinant of success for human kind. Humans should now learn how to produce their food and access medical information is a must for human survival right? The future brings about an existence of personal digital fabrication of goods which will make information the only non-trivial ingredient in substantial good formulation as stated by Captain Capitalism (2020) Information is key!

This current global trend of Company Secrecy should shift towards a trend of Collaborative Information-Rich Sharing Activities which will be exceedingly necessary because sharing information is cost at a non zero-sum, which means that I can give it to you without diminishing my own supply of information. Information determines the production of resources, and if that information is free along with abundant natural ingredients and free available solar energy, then global abundance should be conceivable. If ever the rights to secure and redistribute all natural resources equally amongst humankind was determined by Law. In 2007 a group of business leaders from global companies such as BP; ABB; SUEZ; Infosys; Anglo America; Mckinsey and Alcan met up and set out their views "We believe that we are entering a period of history in which it is becoming clear that the operations of the current system is unsustainable and that progress further tomorrow's global companies need to redefine success and help to create frameworks for the working of the markets.(Tomorrows Company, 2007)

With our current advancement in technologies that we have currently now, we can actually create a world of Abundance Now!!! for all humanity. The Universal free access to information which was secretly held by companies is expected to improve over the course of the next few decades, this should provide the resources for bringing about a high quality source of life to those that are not currently fortunate enough to have the amenities and services of Imperial nations. Worthwhile Social Projects that can enhance humanity societies should be encouraged worldwide, and in fact this applies to First World Countries too as this would cut their Benefit Bill which has instilled inequality and missed opportunities for most Europeans Nationalities too. If the World shared all it's natural resources equally amongst Mankind and if this was enacted in Law too, this will not only provide everyone with the basic necessities for a decent life but give maximum opportunities for people and societies to live and prosper how they might like to be! This means different things to different people. For some it enables a life enhanced by advanced technology, able to do new things they have never been able to before, and for others it means almost the exact opposite allowing them to lead a more basic rural life perhaps within smallholdings, living more in touch with nature and the ability to do this without worrying about money or a bad year in terms of yield from the land or medical care because of the advanced infrastructure in the background that they can call upon if required. Post-scarcity by definition implies 'post-economic' as economics is based on scarcity. Scarcity Economics has made products such as Gold and Diamonds and other raw minerals scarce while they are not scarce materials, I am quite certain that Diamonds and Gold are not rare commodities. In a book titled Economy of Abundance as defined by Stuart Chase(1888-1985) a prominent advisor to the USA Government, he defined the economy of abundance as an economic condition where an abundance of material goods can be produced for the entire population of a given community. However he went on to point out that smooth operations of such an economy is seriously distured when we set technological abundance into a background of prevailing financial habits.

Open your perspectives the world is big and the Universe is bigger. It's amazing to be born at this time because we have to change everything for the better for mankind and not just for a few European Elites. Wake Up World, it's time to think and rethink our lives and where are running to and for what purpose? Why are we chasing paper money to live?.The European elites have used deep psychology to take over our minds they can't own land all over the World. The Church of England, Roman Catholic Church, other European companies own vast acres of land all over the world and Gold too?

I feel it's time the world looked at capitalism with different eyes such as from the eyes of Economics Professor Richard Wolff "Capitalism as a system has spawned deepening economic crises alongside its bought-and-paid-for political establishment. Neither serves the needs of our society. Whether it is secure, well-paid, and meaningful jobs or a sustainable relationship with the natural environment that we depend on, our society is not delivering the results people need and deserve. One key cause for this intolerable state of affairs is the lack of genuine democracy in our economy as well as in our politics. The solution requires the institution of genuine economic democracy, starting with workers managing their own workplaces, as the basis for a genuine political democracy". This was stated by Richard D. Wolff as he laid out a hopeful and concrete vision of how to make that possible, addressing the many people who have concluded economic inequality and politics as usual can no longer be tolerated and are looking for a concrete program of action. "Wolff's constructive and innovative ideas suggest new and promising foundations for much more authentic democracy and sustainable and equitable development, ideas that can be implemented directly and carried forward. A very valuable contribution in troubled times." Noam Chomsky, leading public intellectual and author of *Hope and Prospects*

This current CoronaVirus has brought about a Global Economic Standstill giving Mankind time to rethink their true purpose in life, a chance for a positive restart. These are turbulent times. A quick glance at the headlines is enough to set anybody on edge and with the endless stream that has lately become our lives, it's hard to get away from those headlines. Worse evolution shaped the human brain to be acutely aware of all the potential dangers and thus our News Media and Politicians focus on the grim to capture your mindshare.(Peter.H. Diamonds & Steven Kotler, 2014)

With the advancement in technologies we currently have, we can actually recreate a world of Abundance Now!!! for all humanity...By Vincent Happy Mnisi

Abundance Now!!!

This book Abundance Now!!! will look into Capitalism as it's a predatory system of living and my opinions are now considering Europeans to be a Mental Race for establishing such a Taxing System of living. My thought's for Abundance Now!!! are taking me into weird spheres of views because why establish an Illusive system which is going to be manipulative at every stage from Education, to Business to Religion. They have planned everything for centuries. Like Countries that are part of the Capitalistic systems listed on New York and London Stock exchanges we have to break this European Human Taxing System of Governance ASAP! This project emerged with Enslavement, to Colonisation, to Imperialism which is nevertheless in implementation to this very day. People born with Gold and Diamonds on the soles of their feet are forced to starve and beg for food. Predatory System Capitalism is, humans shouldn't have to need money to survive. This economic system in place is crazy. We have to overhaul everything and get rid of all these predatory Churches and Companies i.e Charities they are the worst criminals. I am still digging deep in my soul for answers why they would indeed continue to go to war for these Capitalistic ideals is indeed more disgraceful to me is how they established Slavery, Colonisations, Imperialism and now Capitalism. We need to recreate life from what we perceive it now. We need to establish a World where everybody lives in abundance and never lacks anything but to seek to discover themselves. Heaven on earth is what we should all wish to recreate life from what we have now. We need to set up a world where everybody lives in abundance and never lacking for anything but seeking to discover themselves, economics shouldn't be the purpose for humans but living life. Capitalism is certainly an anti human concept and we have to eradicate it ASAP. Heaven on earth is what we desire for every individual living in Abundance like the 1% European Aristocracy at the moment my dreams!!!!, "There is more than sufficient wealth to go around and satisfy all of humanity's demands."(V.H Mnisi, 2019)

"Mankind's main purpose on earth is to discover self and to become a purpose for humanity". This book 'Abundance' will investigate how wealth is a false construct and how everybody can live in abundance but due to the Capitalistic Systems in place which has a world of scarcity when there is actually sufficient for everybody to live in abundance....."Our planet produces enough food to nourish its entire population. Yet, tonight, 854 million women, men and children will be going to sleep on an empty stomach." an Address by Dr Jacques Diouf, the Director-General of the Food and Agriculture Organization of the United Nations (FAO) at the World Food Day Ceremony in Rome on October 16, 2007, and we have England with so much Gold but no gold mine?

In a book titled Abundance, *"The Future is better than you think"* by Peter. H. Diamond and Steven Kotler in this book they examined the hard facts, the science and the engineering, the social trends and the economic forces that are rapidly transforming our world. They researched the twentieth Century advancements in technology for which brought about incredible advancements and unspeakable tragedy. The 1918 Influenza epidemic killed fifty million people. World War II killed another Sixty Million. There were tsunamis, hurricanes, earthquakes, fires, floods and even plagues of locusts. Despite such unrest this period also saw infant mortality decrease by 90%. Maternal mortality decreased by 99% and overall, human lifespan increased by more than 100%. At this time the cost of food has dropped thirteenfold, the cost of energy twentyfold and the cost of transportation a hundredfold. Pandemics do not respect borders, terrorist organisations operate on a global scale and overpopulation is everyone's problem, what is the best way to solve these issues? Raise global standards of living. Research shows that the wealthier, more educated and healthier nations,the less violence and civil unrest amongst its populace, and the less likely that unrest will spread across its borders. As such stable governments are better prepared to stop an infectious disease outbreak before it becomes a global pandemic. And as a bonus there are direct correlations between quality of life and population growth rates.(P.H Diamandis & S. Kotler 2014)

Many people think they want to accomplish what other successful people have in life. People often see the surface of worldly achievements, but seldom consider that many of those attainments are constructs of a false world, full of traps and endless enticements that lead to nowhere. People tend to believe they want success, and more toys and things, but when they focus on them, to their bewilderment, those very things move out of their reach. My version of success is that my life is full, purposeful, beautiful and boundless. I attribute this success to my spirituality, my good health, and my community of positive relationships which have all come to me as a creation of choice. Success comes from finding your center and your self; being self-centered in a positive and peaceful way. I have researched Systems of Control and what led to their developments, who and what drove them into practice from Slavery to our current Economic Slave State of Mind and Being. I wanted to find out who drove them into practice and who benefited from their existence. This current Capilaitics System we have in place has been set by tenants that were established by the Roman Catholic Church in the early 1500's. Money shouldn't be a means to an end and not a need for every human being. Every human should be paid by their Tax Systems which their families contribute to through Tax Levies Systems deviced to keep the cash in circulation and to get rid of products from outlets. Money should be made free to Humans as it's a means for eating and living, hence every Human Being deserves to live a life without any strife or want as they should be looked after by their Tax Systems when out of work or even sponsored into their own Business Ventures. People should never be stressed because of Economic Systems.(V.H Mnisi, 2019)

The system within which we currently carry on our economic activity, whether as individuals, or as corporations, is a system based on assumptions of scarcity. Most people including most economists still believe that the primary function of the free market is to allocate scarce resources. Despite the fact that many eminent thinkers have challenged this validity of such assumptions, the economic system remains intact albeit increasingly fragile as does the dominant paradigm of scarcity.(P. Sadler, 2012)

Life should never be about competition but should be about fulfilling your earthly purpose of living a life of love, fulfilling your every Human Need and Human Wants without needing to worry about Economics Scarcity Systems. The Human Being was not born to suffer in the Land of Sunshine, Milk and Honey. We African's have to start thinking of our populations who are now living in abject poverty because of the Capitalistic Systematic Laws in place set by the Europeans ages ago. The Freemasons own the land where the Zimbabwean and South African parliament stand on, crazy stuff! Systems set from Colonial times and Imperial times are still in control of our Independence place of Governance crazy stuff now. This Capitalistic Tax Systematic World we live in now was set to benefit Europe for the entity of life. Property Rights should have been erased and started anew each person allocated a piece of land to own for their family heritages established wherever they want to live in the world. Life should not be full of strife, we are all now Economic Slaves now chasing paper money, we are all playing the game monopoly on a real life scale here without the start-up cash to play the game. Capitalism is another Economic Slavery System built to ensure that large Corporations whose foundations can be traced back to Slavery, Colonisation, Imperialism and Neo-Imperialism Systems will continue to own the Worlds Wealth Systemalically which are in the hands and controlled by European run Companies and Establishments. The current world's biggest Corporations; NGO and Governments have been predominantly led by Europeans who have close ties to one or more Secretive Societies Systems.(V.H Mnisi, 2019)

These Secretive Societies Systems John F Kennedy spoke about in his speech in 1964 appoint Company Directors; Managing Directors of Multinational Companies, NGO's and even select who is going to run for Prime Ministership and Presidency in all countries with a Rothschild Reserve Bank. This Capitalistic Systematic World we live in now is full of Cheats, Scoundrels, Manipulative Individuals and Companies wanting in on the next big idea. They swamp any latest innovation like bees to honey. They break down products and recreate their own brands in order to create competition which is at times very unwarranted behaviour and causes losses for the innovators. Capitalism is just pure evil thievery cunning European Mentally which is to discover lands that people lived in and claim to invent products/services that were already invented by other races. One question I have for the Pro-Capitalist System is "Companies are undying entities if they remain profitable right?" "Why create something that will outlive you amassing Hugh Profits and not giving back to the community that is keeping them profitable?"(V.H Mnisi, 2019)

This World is so inverted that the terrorist is made to look like the good guys and the good guys made to look like the terrorists. American twisted propaganda machine at work here towards its people so they can justify wars imagine going to war against Communism and Islam, And why attack Islamic Countries they are just causing the fight. why? is the question I would love to ask all Americans who hate Communism, why? Capitalism is a worse System Of Control (V.H.Mnisi 2019).There is a clear need to develop a stable social/political framework within which the reduction of inequality can take place. This means tackling the causes of international conflicts, civil war, civil disturbances, genonicide and terrorism.(P. Sadler, 2014)

In today's hyperlinked internet world, solving problems anywhere, solved problems everywhere. Moreover the greatest tool we have tackling our grand challenges is the passionate and the dedicated human mind. The information and communications revolution now underway is rapidly spreading across the planet. In 2010 we had just under 2 billion people connected to the internet. By 2020 that number will rise to about 5 billion. Over there next six years, three billion people, new individuals, will be coming online, joining the global conversation and contributing to the global economy. Their ideas were never before had will result in new discoveries, products and inventions that will benefit us all. (P.H.Diamandis & S Kotler, 2014)

Money shouldn't be a thing to have for a decent living, money should be given out for free by all governments as they should make sure that all their citizens are housed, fed and clothed too. Especially with the Automatisation of Industries which is soon to hit the World. I propose that all companies should issue 20% shares to their Workers in their Annual Profits. My argument is that Workers contribute as much as the owners to make sure that the company remains profitable right? and hence should be rewarded profitably accordingly. Work is an Economic Slavery System in disguise and now everybody in the world is out to get themselves as much Worthless Monoply Paper they can get hold off "Money", That has to get paid into a Bank Account and that Money is then used by the Bankers to make more Money from their Money they must deposit into their Banks, this World is a Systematic Bankers Paradise and they are the only ones profiting from everybody that is living today.(V.H Mnisi, 2019)

Inflation is another made up Fallacy System. My visit to South Africa in 2015 was shocking for me to find that they had priced their bread at R10 from the R2 when I was last there in 2002, come on? The price of growing wheat never changes right? and they are still paying low wages and it's a Mass Produced Product and Distributed in bulk too, then what is the excuse of making such a price? The South African Financial Auditors need to check their books because it seems like they are making 1000% profits from a subsistence product which should be made as cheap as possible. The problem is that all companies in South Africa are pegging their prices with the Pound and what you buy for 1 pound in England it's worth R18 in South Africa which is fraud the financial regulators are sleeping in South Africa.(V.H Mnisi, 2019)

I also noted that each commodity in South Africa as priced in shops now each have the petrol price added upon it as though each product travels into the shops alone and not in bulk. One Principle of Business I question is the Prices Escalation of Demand Theory, and the Scarcity of Goods Theory of Driving Up Prices. All these are man-made Capitalistic Systems of Business which has made Capitalistic European Markets able to hoard products such as Diamonds and Gold which are not rare but plentiful in Africa. All African Commodities are traded and controlled from Europe, The Gold Market, The Diamond Market; Flower Markets; Cocco Market; and all African Minerals are priced in Europe. Africa is not in control of its natural resources in the same manner Europe or Asia does, The Middle East and Asia control theirs, that's for sure. How can Africans be born with such riches at the soles of their feet, grow up poor and are always chasing after European Paper Money? The Middle East has set a precedent by Nationalising all their Oil Reserves, Africa should Nationalise all Mineral Resources for the benefit of Africans today and tomorrow. Europeans have used Reverse Psychology Systems of Manipulative Systems into Making Africans Demand their Monopoly Money in exchange for African Raw Minerals. Before granting Independence in each African Country their Resources were purposely sold off to private entities with their UN; IMF and the World Bank offering crippling loans to the New Nationalist against their resources no wonder countries like Zimbabwe and Zambia were crippled when they had arguments with their Reserves Bank owners The Rothschilds and Co. Hence the Rothschilds began printing ridiculous notes such as 1 Million Zimbabwe Dollar notes and the Zambian 1 million Kwacha too. Their currencies were taken to the mud when Kaunda and Mugabe tried to get rid of the Rothschild Debit Reserve Banking Systems from owning their Resources and Usury Reserve Bank Systems.(V.H Mnisi, 2019)

This European's Capitalistic System has allowed them to steal and innovate other people's ideas and religious doctrines all in the name of Capitalism. The backbone of Capitalism in its current form was built by the theft of African Slaves by the Freemasons; Colonialism; Imperialism; Neo-Imperialism and now Fake Independences granted to African countries while the Europeans have full control of the Economies of every African state even printing their monies for their Ex-French Colonies and still in charge of all the other Reserve Banking Systems of the World too. The Rothchild family has a stack in every currency that is being printed in Africa and can make or break it in the World Currency Market System as they control the London Currency Exchange where Currencies values are decided. Capitalism when looked at it Socially is an Exploitative Human System. Its general makeup and after some analysis, I have realised that my education was Systemically Capitalistically Inclined as my Studies of Advertising and Business and practicing as an Advertising Executive concluded to me that Businesses are an Exploitative Set of Systems setup to Exploit Markets because of the Demand for their products they create Demand for through Advertising and Marketing Activities.(V.H Mnisi, 2019)

Robert Theobald, an English Economist who moved to the United States in the 1950's once pointed out in his book "*The challenge of Abundance*" that the rules of our systems depended upon the assumptions of scarcity. He argued that the stage of abundance is reached when the increase in the production of material goods raises new problems even while meeting the traditional goal of a higher material standard of living. He viewed the development of high-production, high consumptions, economy makes it necessary to re-examine certain basic economic theories by which we lived in the past. He stated that "In an economy of abundance, economic growth would not need to be given top priority, science could be used in such a way that it could increase rather than decrease the validity of human life. Similarly we would need to re-examine the belief that the invisible hand of economic forces will automatically lead to a coincidence between private and social goals". Theobald questioned and criticized conventional confidence in economic growth, in technology, and in the culture of materialism all of which he considered to be damaging to the environment while failing to provide opportunity and income for many of the world's people. He warned against trying to maintain, and to spread or mimic worldwide, the American standard of living of the late 20th century. Despite his criticism of some aspects and effects of technology, Theobald saw tremendous potential in communications technology like on-line, personal computers which in the 1980s he termed "micro-computers", seeing these as tools for pooling the thoughts and opinions of very large numbers of individuals spread widely, geographically. Theobald was an expositor and popularizer of such now-accepted concepts as "networking," "win/win," "systemic thinking," and "communications era."

Structural Economist Prebisch (1950) argued in his book that long-run decline in the primary export is an inevitable result of the increasing use of synthetics which is shrinking the need for raw materials causing a low elasticity of demand for raw materials inturn. Also Prebisch also stated that the Oligopolistic markets in the industrial countries meant that productivity increase there were captured in the form of higher income for workers and owners whereas in developing countries productivity gains were passed on to consumers in the turn of lower prices in turn creating a consumer market which Africans have become. Prebisch also projected a downward trend in the terms of trade from primary commodities in relation to manufactured goods imported by the developing countries Prebich urged the reduced dependency on exporting primary commodities in favour of heavy investment in the manufacturing aimed initially at supplying their domestic markets. The rights to Africa's Mineral Wealth are now in the hands of European, American and Chinese Investors who are making a killing from exploiting African Rich Mineral Deposits. One sad fact and example is Zambia selling of their Copper deposit to a private Company Glencore which is also owned by the Rothschild family who have made a killing from it and have not yet paid their appropriate taxes that they are supposed to pay and their extraction methods have also caused illnesses to the community living close to their mine too.

Glencore are still involved with a lot of controversies all over the world, but most notably in Africa like the Congo where their Luilu copper refinery pumps acid into the rivers and Zambia where their Mopani mine is polluting the air with Sulphur Oxides.(V.H Mnisi, 2019) Zambia is now owned by China.

France's presence in Africa is focused largely on its former colonies. During a painful process of decolonization in the 1960s and 1970s, "La Grande Nation " never lost sight of its own interest in Africa. The use of the French language in the former French territories remains Systematically Obligatory and French African's are very proud of their French Heritage. There is a Two Currency Union System in existence the West African CFA Franc and the Central African CFA Franc to which a total of 15 African states belong. All Currency Reserves and Gold are held in France's Central Banking Systems. Is it open to dispute whether the CFA offers greater advantages to France or the African States? French corporations such as the construction company Bolloré, the Oil giant Total and the telecoms group Orange maintain a massive presence in the ex-colonies. Stefan Brüne, an expert on Franco-African relations at the German Council on Foreign Relations in Berlin, believes nonetheless that French influence in Africa may be waning slightly, but it is still very much in evidence. There are still strong links between Paris and the former colonies," he said French companies import raw commodities from many West and Central African Countries, such as Uranium ore from Niger and Gabon or Cocoa from the Ivory Coast. About 9,000 French soldiers are stationed in those countries. Their mandate is to fight terrorists and train African troops but it seems like they are there to protect French interests in the region. As stated before European; American and Chinese Economic Systems are now heavily dependent on their Systematic Exploitative Mineral Rights that they have in Africa through their Multinational Companies which are controlled by the Freemason's; Skull and Bones and Illuminati Graduates. Graduates from these Secretive Societies Systems are appointed to Political; Business and Religious positions of power and I shall go into more detail later in the book. Quite relevant to all this, I have made several points above. One was that, notwithstanding the European Well-Developed Systems of maintaining disunity within the African Race, Europeans are still disturbed by any signs of any movement towards unity amongst African Governing Systems and go into action in many subtle ways to offset it and stop the African Awakening.(V.H Mnisi,2019)

The IMF and the World Bank work to ensure that African countries are constantly in debt. In addition with the extensive Inter African trade envisaged from the signing of the Inter The African Continental Free Trade Area (AfCFTA) which was signed by 44 African Countries at a summit of the African Union in Kigali, Rwanda which will attracts foriegn investment and modern technology and growth is therefore maximised by ensuring the maintenance of free internal and external markets for goods and should also be allocating capital resources to the populations in the free capital resources to the people in free capital markets. This must be made possible from the age of 18 plus Africans must be taught to be self reliant. Africa needs a Rigorous Social Service System that will uplift and look after its populations from Cape to Cario. This view is opposed by the current economic structure in place with multinational owning mineral rights in Africa and the divide and rule regiment currently in place in Africa.(V.H Mnisi, 2015)

African Governments should favour forward planning and the setting up non-market allocation of resources through a variety of controls and government incentives for prices for domestic and foriegn trade structures. The Foriegn Exchange System will need to be sterilized in order for the local currencies to appreciate in demand. The need for foriegn currency should be minimised and countries should swap goods for goods. This will bring about an increase of locally produced commodities competing with imported commodities, the domestic products will increase in demand as their prices will be much lower than imported goods. The manufacturing of products versus importing for resource abundant countries with different natural resources endowment is vital for the local community to build local enterprises which can be set up to be taxable companies too.

In a Post scarcity society the society of abundance in which scarcity has been eliminated, envisaged by some socialist thinkers. Counter-arguments suggest that there are always likely to be some scarcities given that world resources are finite. A postindustrial, or postmodern, order might arise where the impetus to continuous accumulation associated with CAPITALISM was replaced by other goals in life, and it is in this sense that endemic scarcity might then cease, In the Free Trade negotiations launched in June 2011 between the SADC, Common Market for Eastern and Southern Africa (COMESA) and the East Africa countries would open up a market of US 1.3 trillion in terms of the Gross Domestic Product." SADC Common Market and COMESA Market Claudia Furriel a Director of the New Partnership for Africa's Development (NEPAD) at the Department of Trade and Industry (dti) Conference stated that the continent's free trade agreements, particularly the Tripartite Free Trade Agreement and the envisaged Continental Free Trade Area present an opportunity for African countries to improve intra-regional trade and diversify Africa's current trade model of exporting raw materials and importing of finished products.

"In addition, the continental free trade that is to be established with 55 countries and a GDP of US 2.6 trillion presents an opportunity to access greater markets. On this free trade agreement, we are not only looking at trade in goods but also trade in services. Market integration, supported by infrastructure development and industrial development, will enable Africa to become competitive and benefit from other trade agreements with other partners," said Furriel. Furriel told delegates at the conference the continent's full potential will remain unfulfilled unless challenges of poor infrastructure, small and fragmented markets, under-developed production structures and inadequate economic transformation are addressed. "Regional integration is an important aspiration of the African Union's Agenda 2063 and remains a critical component of the continent's efforts to ensure sustainable economic development and inclusive growth through the creation of a larger regional market and improving Africa's integration in the global economy, "She stated at the Dti Conference as stated in a Journal AGOA Africa Growth and Opportunity Act.

The African Continental Free Trade Area (AfCFTA) has been finally signed by all African Countries with Nigeria finally signing it on the 8th of July 2019 this a step forward to economic integration and for the African Union to achieve it's 2063 Agenda closer for African total integration, 27 member states also signed their commitment for the free movement of persons. 2063 is a bit too far. Africa needs one GDP's now in earnest and should form one African Currency ASAP as suggested in my African Unity books. 2063 is too far and it should be brought to a closer date I suggest by 2030. This African Political and Economic Unity will not only benefit International traders but will uplift the African community by having one single currency making it easier for trading. The current currency market of the 54 different currencies currently in circulation in Africa which are not even worth rating individually when comparing them to International currencies. The Current Digital Banking Systems in-place in Africa can form the bridge for International Digital Marketers, the Eastern Africa M-Pesa banking system has revolutionised the way money is transferred and banked.It has also transformed Banking internationally and they should be credited for this incredible innovation.

Despite the IMF and the World Bank working constantly to ensure that African countries are constantly in debt. The future for Africa seems brighter with singing of the extensive Inter African trade envisaged from the Inter The African Continental Free Trade Area (AfCFTA) which was signed by 44 African Countries at a summit of the African Union in Kigali, Rwanda which will attracts foriegn investment and modern technology and growth is therefore maximised by ensuring the maintenance of free internal and external markets for goods and should also be allocating capital resources to the populations in the free capital resources to the people in free capital markets. This must be made possible from the age of 18 plus Africans must be taught to be self reliant. Africa needs a Rigorous Social Service System that will uplift and look after its populations from Cape to Cario.

This view is opposed by the current economic structure in place with multinational owning mineral rights in Africa and the divide and rule regiment currently in place in Africa. African Governments should favour forward planning and the setting up non-market allocation of resources through a variety of controls and government incentives for prices for domestic and foriegn trade structures. Europeans have got it to a fine T with their Social Services Grants Systems in place were every 18 plus earns from their Unemployment Benefit Funds (UB40) and everyone in Europe gets paid monthly enough to live on and Africa needs to play catch up, by looking after our populations too and then our population will become self-reliant with Social Systems in place which will aid them to become more Industrusruous. Why have Europeans always hated Communism, I wonder why? Capitalism is built on Competition on who is the best in Class, at Sport, Speaking, Cheating etc. Why create a Competitive Social Environment where people have to compete to seem normal? meaning to be better than normal you have to be number one in a specific field of study or overstanding. Everyone is created differently and we all react differently to everything we learn and our perceptions and interpretations will be different for each individual. Hence I do believe that the current Grading Systems in schools undermine the overstandings of different interpretations from each individual's perceptions or it lacks to correct it when the subject is misunderstood too.(V.H Mnisi, 2019)

This current wealth gathering Systematic Driven World is only but just an illusion because wealth are earthly things and shall be left behind when we pass on to the next Life System. Human Beings main pursuit on earth should be to Understand Self and to Overstand their Connection with their Creator by finding their own gifts within which will make them Creative Human Beings that we were born to become. Everyone is born with a Spiritual System within learning to connect with it through Meditation and Solitude should be your goal. The World Environmental Systems are another concern, Global warming caused by pollution from Industrious Countries needs to be addressed ASAP. Take a look at the temperature of the North Pole now? Scary! I must say and if the World gets just another 4% hotter London and New York will be underwater. 5G is another worrying point, this technology we are all embracing will be our downfall mark my words. At least this quarantine now gives you time to yourself for once to reflect upon your life and where is it leading to.(V.H.Mnisi, 2019)

Africa needs to unite NOW!!! economically at least we need to form a United Gross Domestic Product (GDP) in-order for Africa to form one currency which will compete against the Euro; £ and the USA$ in the world markets because Africa holds most of the natural resources the world needs today. Africa has a rich cultural heritage of UBUNTU, we Africans need to socialize in order to grow in the arts and music. We have to start setting targets to achieve Millennium Development Goals which will fulfill African Societies aims. Africa Must Unite for the betterment of its people in-order to consolidate Africa's natural resources.

According to a McKinsey report, the continent's consumer-facing industries are expected to grow by $400 billion by 2020. Africa's new class of consumers has a smaller family, is better educated, often lives in cities and is digitally savvy. It is also the fastest growing and youngest in the world and looks very different from Asia or America. The typical African customer in Nairobi, Lagos or Johannesburg pays for their solar electricity with mobile money. Farmers check the weather, the news or watch TV on their smartphones and communicate with their buyers over whatsapp. Over the next five years, GSMA reckons that the continent will house 725 million unique mobile subscribers with the majority based in Nigeria, Egypt, South Africa, Ethiopia and Tanzania. The same report finds that in 2015, mobile technologies and services generated 6.7% of GDP in Africa, a contribution that amounted to around $150 billion of economic values into their respective Countries GDP contributions. Africa needs to combine their GDP to enable them to form One African Currency as stated in the African Unity books I have published. "Africa Must Unite"; "The United Countries of Africa Now!!!" and "My African Black Book " these books are available from Amazon.

"Stats leaves no room for doubt; Africa represents a huge growth market and technology and innovation will underpin its digital revolution. As usual, Google is at the forefront of these efforts: in 2016 it has already trained about 1 million Africans to gain terms of digital skills! The Google's Digital Skills Program offers 89 courses that can be taken online or offline to help mostly young people across Africa better understand how to take advantage of the web. For the offline part, Google works with 14 partners across many countries in Africa" stated by Gori Yahaya in an article titled "*Africa The Next Frontier For Digital Marketers*" African economies have the biggest potential for rapid growth due to the fact that most of them also have ample cropland to grow their own food and why Africa is still importing food is amazing to me? Africa should use their mineral exports to further enhance their capacity both to invest and to import compared with the non mineral economies. African Governments have to Nationalise all mineral mining resources for the benefit of its citizens to consolidate the wealth they are born with. The disappointing points of performances of the resource abundant countries appears to be robust with regard to the differences in the classification of the natural resource endowment as there is no consensus on the measurement of resource abundance.(Prebisch,1950).

There is controversy among developed countries concerning the contribution of primary commodities from underdeveloped countries in their early stages of development which can generate the foriegn currency necessary to pay for essential imports and also to service their external debts imposed to keep developing countries in bondage (Prebisch,1950). The IMF and the World Bank work to ensure that African countries are constantly in debt. Africa must fight back by building extensive Inter African trade which will attracts foriegn investment and modern technology, Growth is therefore maximised by ensuring the maintenance of free internal and external markets for goods and by also allocating capital resources to the populations in the free capital resources to the people in free capital markets.

This must be made possible from the age of 18 plus. Africa needs a Social Service System to look after its populations from Cape to Cario. This view is opposed by the current economic structure. African Governments should favour the planning and the setting up non-market allocation of resources through a variety of controls and government incentives for prices for domestic and foriegn trade structures. Structural economist Prebisch (1950) argued in his book that long-run decline in the primary export is an inevitable result of the increasing use of synthetics which is shrinking the need for raw materials causing a low elasticity of demand for raw materials inturn. Also Prebisch also stated that the Oligopolistic markets in the industrial countries meant that productivity increase there were captured in the form of higher income for workers and owners whereas in developing countries productivity gains were passed on to consumers in the turn of lower prices in turn creating a consumer market which Africans have become, by decentralizing production of these things will also allow more equal access to them and sidestep many of the issues involved in distributing them. These methods could overcome nearly all significant scarcity that persists due to the economic framework we have inherited from previous eras.

One scarce resource today for people is time. In a post-scarcity culture, not having to spend the best part of the day working for a living also frees people up to spend more time with each other, something that is vital for a proper community. Both for friendship and mentoring the next generation. However some people feel that increasing automation is a threat. A threat to their livelihoods, a threat to humanity's pride even. The reality is that automation is likely to provide in scenarios where people would prefer not to do that job. It leaves people free to be creative and industrious in activities that they want to be part of and allows for greater variety than the average working life offers today. The mobile-ecosystem has been identified as a leading contributor to the growth of Africa's economy according to data collected by Infinite Potentials, a professional services consulting firm. Their report further stated that mobile technologies and services had generated approximately US$ 152 billion of economic value in Africa in 2015. This is expected to increase by about 41% by 2020 to US$ 215 billion. Open design will enable people to be involved in the creation or customisation of the goods they want in a way not seen before and reverses the trend of people simply being passive consumers. Creativity is something that can give huge satisfaction to people but if not fulfilled can cause great frustration and dissatisfaction. It enables an individual to have more control over their environment and life. In recent decades resource-abundant developing countries have been underperforming in creating an abundant life for their citizens, when compared with resource-deficient developed countries due to the post colonial and current imperial measures in place benefiting Europe and European companies as they have still maintained private ownership of the mineral rights in the name of capitalism i.e De Beers and Anglo American still own mining rights in Africa post Independence.

Prebisch also stated that the Oligopolistic markets in the industrial countries meant that productivity increase there were captured in the form of higher income for workers and owners whereas in developing countries productivity gains were passed on to consumers in the turn of lower prices in turn creating a consumer market which Africans have become, by decentralizing production of these things will also allow more equal access to them and sidestep many of the issues involved in distributing them. These methods could overcome nearly all significant scarcity that persists due to the economic framework we have inherited from previous eras. As Structural Economist Prebisch(1950) argued in his book that long-run decline in the primary export is an inevitable result of the increasing use of synthetics which is shrinking the need for raw materials causing a low elasticity of demand for raw materials inturn. Also Prebisch also stated that the Oligopolistic markets in the industrial countries meant that productivity increase there were captured in the form of higher income for workers and owners whereas in developing countries productivity gains were passed on to consumers in the turn of lower prices in turn creating a consumer market which Africans have become.

Prebisch projected a downward trend in the terms of trade from primary commodities in relation to manufactured goods imported by the developing countries Prebich urged the reduced dependency on exporting primary commodities in favour of heavy investment in the manufacturing aimed initially at supplying their domestic markets. This isn't to say what is proposed here may happen, but that it could happen it is feasible from a physical and technological viewpoint today. It is a matter of spreading the knowledge that these things are possible and enough people choosing to work towards it. Post-scarcity is a theoretical economic situation in which most goods can be produced in great abundance with minimal human labor needed, so that they become available to all very cheaply or even freely. Structural economist Prebisch (1950) also argued in his book that long-run decline in the primary export is an inevitable result of the increasing use of synthetics which is shrinking the need for raw materials causing a low elasticity of demand for raw materials inturn.

Stuart Chase wrote in a book titled *"The Affluent Society"* published in 1969 where he pointed out problems that have had traditional economists in the previous centuries like Smith; Ricardo and Malthus based their theories in a world characterised by poverty. He maintained that the problem of production had been solved that all citizens could have enough to satisfy their needs and output if it was distributed more equally. He stated that a lot of what America produced was wasteful i.e oversized cars. In a post-scarcity abundant world society means that the basic necessities of living will be available for everyone who requires it. As normal they will be markets for certain goods that can be purposefully made publicly not available or are rare in nature. The important point here about post-scarcity is that for the first time the general population will be able to live comfortably without having to owe anyone else their time. People will not have to suffer from drudgery work which amounts to a wage slavery system during the best years of their lives. Unfortunately but true that most people today in both white and blue collar jobs would really rather be doing something else with their time than the jobs they are employed to do.

Work is economic slavery esepcially when you feel like what you are doing is not directly relevant to your life or is not particularly interesting and feel you are simply a cog in the system with little control. Currently we all have to be active in the employment markets so as to afford food, shelter and goods. While in a post-scarcity abundant society which will enable mankind to have more time and space to work on things that are important to them, and to learn the skills needed to reach their goals and have room to be more creative. One very scarce resource we have today for people is time. In the envisaged post-scarcity culture, not having to spend the best part of the day working for a living also frees people up to spend more time with each other, something that is vital for a proper community. Both for friendship and mentoring the next generation. However some people feel that increasing automation is a threat to human dignity of needing to work or a threat to their livelihoods, and even a threat to humanity's pride.

The reality is that automation will hopefully provide a scenario where people would prefer not to do that job in the first place. That's if this is managed and funded properly by Governments it will leave people free to be creative and industrious in activities that they want to be part of and allows for greater variety than the average working life offered today. Post-scarcity does not mean that scarcity has been eliminated for all goods and services, but that all people can easily have their basic survival needs met along with some significant proportion of their desires for goods and services. Writers on the topic often emphasize that some commodities will remain scarce in a post-scarcity society. With this current CoronaVirus COVID19 that has hit the world in 2020, this virus has made Mankind rethink their purpose in life. Humans should learn to overstand that they have been trained to do their jobs and that they are not their jobs. This is the time to reflect and and to try to overstand what your true purpose on earth is? As far as I am concerned this virus was created by humans to kill humans, that's my take on things don't take my word for it. Each Government now has the chance to make everyone of its citizens to be self sustainable and self reliant on their food sources too. There is so much land that can be shared equally. With the current technologies in place humans don't need to congregate in cities in search for work, humans can now live in rural settings and still stay connected to the wider world. Customer open design innovations will enable consumers to be involved in the creation or customisation of the goods they want in a way not seen before and reverses the trends of humankind being passive consumers. Creativity is something that can give huge satisfaction to people but if not fulfilled can cause great frustration and dissatisfaction. Creativity enables individuals to have more control over their environment and life. In recent decades resource-abundant developing countries have been underperforming in creating an abundant life for their citizens, when compared with resource-deficient developed countries due to the post colonial and current imperial measures in place benefiting Europe and European companies as they have still maintained private ownership of the mineral rights in the name of Capitalism.

De Beers owns the rights to Diamonds worldwide and Anglo American still owns mining rights in Africa post-Independence. African Economies have the biggest potential for rapid growth due to the fact that most of them also have ample cropland to grow their own food and why Africa is still importing food is amazing to me? Africa should use their mineral exports to further enhance their capacity both to invest and to import compared with the non mineral economies. African Governments have to Nationalise all mineral mining resources for the benefit of its citizens to consolidate the wealth they are born with. The disappointing points of performances of the resource abundant countries appears to be robust with regard to the differences in the classification of the natural resource endowment as there is no consensus on the measurement of resource abundance. (Prebisch,1950). The best manner of protest against Capitalism is by not participating in it as a slave but as a creator. Every Human is born with a jewel inside of them, and needs to learn to use it by self-discovery through mediation. Discover your purpose you were not born with riches for at the soles of your feet for no reason. All Africans should be Millionaires if the wealth was shared out equally.

"Some become dishonest intellectuals for they see the irrationalities of capitalism but enjoy its benefit's way of life for their own selfish reasons are prepared to prostitute themselves and become agents and supporters of privilege reaction"...By Kwame Krumah

The Post-Scarcity Anarchism

In a book entitled Post-Scarcity Anarchism by Murray Bookchin, in his 1971 essay collection Post-Scarcity Anarchism, in this book he described an post-economic society which was based on social conservation, libertarian municipalism, and an abundance of fundamental resources, suggesting that post-industrial communities have the potential to be developed into post-scarcity societies. For Bookchin, such improvement would implement "the fulfillment of the social and cultural potentialities inherent in a technology of abundance". Bookchin claimed that the expanded production made possible by the technological advances of the twentieth century were in the pursuit of market profit and at the expense of the needs of humans and of ecological sustainability.

The post-scarcity age is an anticipated period where due to advancing technology which is available today and the efficient use of natural resources which belong to all mankind and mutual cooperation between companies there should exist a great abundance of the material items that everyone needs, achieved with a minimal impact to the environment. Many fictional visions and versions of post scarcity involve yet undeveloped technologies but the reality is that global material abundance can be produced with our current technologies. Food is one example, where there is more than enough produced for everyone on the planet but due to politics, economics and logistics this prevents fair distribution to all mankind allowing it to go to waste instead. The bottom line is that in the fundamental resources of this planet there exists for all mankind and there magnitude of abundant natural energy, raw material and biological resources than humanity requires, it is a matter of developing systems that can be used and distribute them more efficiently within mankind. By employing open collaborative design, digital manufacturing and advanced automation in combination, everything we need should be trivial. Mankind should be able to self fabricate and share basic things such as clean water, good quality food, medecine and suitable housing for all mankind, to increasingly essential material goods such as electric vehicles for all, computers and mobile phones all the way up to purely luxury items. By decentralizing production of these things will also allow more equal access to them and sidestep many of the issues involved in distributing them. These methods could overcome nearly all significant world scarcity that persists due to the economic framework we have inherited from previous eras. This isn't to say what is proposed here will happen, but that it could happen and is feasible from a physical and technological viewpoint. It is a matter of spreading the knowledge that these things are possible and enough people choosing to work towards having Post-scarcity not in a theoretical economic situation but with a drive to produce in great abundance with minimal human labor needed, so that they become available to all very cheaply or even freely. Post-scarcity does not mean that scarcity has been eliminated for all goods and services, but that all people can easily have their basic survival needs met along with some significant proportion of their desires for goods and services. Writers on the topic often emphasize that some commodities will remain scarce in a post-scarcity society.(M. Bookchin, 1971)

In the Post-Scarcity Article by Posted by Captain Capitalism in March 2020, he went state that the accumulation of money can no longer be recognized as essential for individual emancipation, and the notion that obstructions such as the state, social hierarchy, and vanguard political parties are necessary in the striving for freedom of the working classes can be eliminated as a myth. This portrayal is based on an alternative series of presumptions to those most consistently held about human nature and the corollary approach to political and economic life. Ideas are gathered from two collections of philosophers, each writing respectively at the change of the last two centuries. As both historical periods are marked by challenges of progressivism, the reconceptualization is formulated around an alternative awareness of "progress" and exploration of a political economy that would bolster this different explanation. Specifically, in a comparative rather than material recognition of progress, community administration would be remodeled into a process of self-governance within political and economic systems based on assumptions of generative rather than degenerative principles that replace fear with love, scarcity with abundance, self-interest with collective interest, and dialectical competition and hierarchy with collaboration. Although this might sound utopian at face value, no such conceptions of accomplishment are expected. Rather, the systems of progress collaboration and co-creation are commonly presumed to be possible and the precise basis for civil institutions undertaking to foster them. This reconceptualization offers a transformative role for public administration in urging a unique definition of progress, co-established political democracy, democratizing the economy, and shifting the role of government, in addition to a facilitative role in the emerging political economy.

In yet another journal entitled "The Post-Scarcity World of 2050–2075" by Tim Adams, Tim Adams argues that we are presently living in an age of scarcity arising from inadvertent conduct as concerns the future of the 19th and 20th centuries. The era between 1975 and 2005 which was marked by relative abundance because of colonised resources   such as oil, water, energy, food, credit, etc which encouraged industrialization and development in the Western Economies. An enhanced requirement of resources merged with a soaring population brought to resource exhaustion. In part, the theories developed about post-scarcity are propelled by analyses that hypothesize that capitalism leverages scarcity. One of the main traces of the scarcity periods is the increase and fluctuation of prices. Made up inflation. In order to deal with the present situation, advancement in technologies will perform a significant role and facilitate efficient usage of resources to a definite amount that costs will be substantially diminished and practically everything will be free. Consequently, some authors assert that the age between 2050 and 2075 will be a post-scarcity age in which scarcity will no longer exist. An ideological contradiction to the post-scarcity economy is established by the approach of a stable-state economy.

The significance of such findings, that underdevelopment of all kinds literally reduces vision and the ingenuity to construct one's own life, are suggested as somewhat radical. As antidotes the authors suggest a sequence of nudge-related interventions to "create bandwidth" for the time-poor these can be as simple as setting up direct debits, for the cash-poor it might involve providing some kind of insurance against "small shocks", a puncture, a sick cow, a rent rise that can lead to moneylenders and loan sharks, or providing proper working days rather than the debilitating stress of Zero-Hours Contracts. Such solutions are hardly news. Neither, you imagine, will the case that compelling need limits long-term prospects and self-regulation come as a disturbance to anyone but the idle rich and the government.

This "scarcity trap" furnishes a description for unpleasant facts, most authors suggest. It explains why the "poor are more prone to be obese and they are less likely to send their children to school… why? the poorest in a village are the ones least likely to wash up their hands or treat their water before consuming it." And the explanation is this: "the poor are not just short of cash. They are short on bandwidth." When an individual or any human being is primed to think about his money concerns, his capacity to execute assessments and tasks is somewhat decreased. Reminded that they are poor, individuals "appeared less flexible intellect, less executive command. With scarcity on his mind, he barely had less mind for everything else.".."In a world increasingly polarised by wealth, the resolutions to uncover a metaphor that unifies rich and poor, a divided humanity, if you felt like, has become both a profitable and a somewhat desperate publishing venture. Most of the academic traffic is focused at the busy crossroads between economics and psychology, where a nudge is as efficient as a flash. The suggestion that we are characterized by and subject matter to market pressures is drawn as a presented in this work; the interest exists in the disparity between the economist's faith in intelligent decision-making and the psychologist's stacked-up evidence of our less than rational behaviours: in the disclosure of our almost comical inability to assume risk and reward and to achieve what is best for us. Post scarcity or post-scarcity Economies depicts a theoretical construct of economy or society, regularly explored in science fiction, in which objects such as goods, services and information are free, or essentially free. This would be due to an abundance of fundamental resources matter, energy and intellect, in partnership with sophisticated computerized systems capable of transforming raw materials into completed goods, providing manufacturing to be as easy as duplicating software. Even without postulating new technologies, it is conceivable that previously there remains enough energy, raw materials and biological resources to provide a comfortable lifestyle for every person on Earth. However indeed a hypothetical political or economic system effective to solve an equitable distribution of goods would generally not be described as a "post-scarcity society" unless the production of goods was sufficiently automated that essentially no labour was required by anyone. It is normally presumed there would even be enough of voluntary creative labour, such as a writer creating a novel or a software engineer working on open-source software.

There are some anomalies to this usage of Post-Scarcity. Anthony Giddens, for example, applies "post-scarcity" to deal with a series of trends he shows that in contemporary industrialized communities, such as an enhanced focus on "life politics" and a diminished focus on productivity and economic expansion. Giddens recognized that the term has still been applied historically to mean an actual end of scarcity. The term post-scarcity economics is somewhat of a misnomer because scarcity is a characterizing component of current economics. Quoting a 1932 essay composed by Lionel Robbins, economics is: "the science which investigates human behaviour as a relationship between ends and limited means which have alternative uses Today, futurists who speak of "post-scarcity" suggest economies based on advances in automated manufacturing technologies, generally incorporating the perception of self-replicating machines, the adoption of division of labour which in theory could produce practically all goods in abundance, produced adequate raw materials and energy. More speculative constructs of nanotechnology such as molecular assemblers or nanofactories, which do not presently exist suggest the possibility of devices that can automatically manufacture any specified goods given the correct instructions and the necessary raw materials and energy, and then many nanotechnology enthusiasts have proposed it will initiate in a post-scarcity world. In the imminent-term future, the increasing automation of physical labor using robots is repeatedly considered as an instrument of creating a post-scarcity economy.

Increasingly adaptable plans for rapid prototyping machines, and a hypothetical self-replicating adaptation of such an apparatus established as a RepRap, have further been anticipated to facilitate set up the abundance of goods required for a post-scarcity economy. Advocates of self-replicating machines such as Adrian Bowyer, the founder of the RepRap project, suggests that once a self-replicating apparatus is produced, then since anyone who controls one can make more copies to sell and would likewise be free to request for a lower price than alternative marketers. Market competition will naturally drive the cost of such machines down to the bare minimum required to make a profit, in this instance just above the cost of the physical materials and energy that must be supplied into the system as input, and the same should go for any other goods that the instrument can produce. Even with totally automated production, limitations on the amount of goods manufactured would result from the availability of raw materials and energy, as well as ecological damage correlated with manufacturing technologies. Advocates of technological abundance often argue for more comprehensive adoption of renewable energy and better recycling in conduct to prevent future reductions in availability of energy and raw materials, and low ecological disturbance. Solar energy in specific is repeatedly emphasized, as the cost of solar panels continues to drop and could drop far more with automated production by self-replicating machines, and advocates point out the total solar energy striking the Earth's surface annually exceeds our civilization's present annual energy usage by a factor of thousands.

Most conceptions of post-scarcity societies expect the reality of new technologies which make it often smoother for society to produce virtually all goods in extreme abundance, given raw materials and energy are free. More speculative constructs of nanotechnology (such as molecular assemblers or nanofactories) establish the possibility of devices that can automatically manufacture any specified goods given the correct instructions and the necessary raw materials and energy. Even before that achievement of automation can be obtained, fab labs and developed industrial automation might be effective to produce most physical goods that people seek, with a minimum amount of human labour required. As for the free raw materials and energy required as encouragement for such automated production processes, self-replicating automated mining plants set loose in the world or other sections of territory with vast volumes of untapped raw materials could lead to the prices of these materials to decline. New energy sources such as synthesis energy or solar power satellites could do the same for energy, especially if the power plants/power satellites could themselves be constructed in an exceptionally automated approach, so their quantity would be curbed only by raw materials and energy as stated in the Post-Scarcity Article by Posted by Captain Capitalism

"In the long run, making programs free is a step toward the post-scarcity world, where nobody will have to work very hard just to make a living. People will be free to devote themselves to activities that are fun, such as programming, after spending the necessary ten hours a week on required tasks such as legislation, family counselling, robot repair and asteroid prospecting. There will be no need to be able to make a living from programming."...(Unknown)

Market economies or planned economies may be irrelevant in a post-scarcity age, even though grant or exchange economies may hold their place once the scarcity driving earlier types of economy disappears. Post-scarcity societies might likewise have their market economies restricted to the exchange of energy and resources, or of other sparse or indeed non-material factors, such as prominence or stature, real estate, or skills and expertise. In Wealth, Virtual Wealth and Debt (George Allen & Unwin 1926), Frederick Soddy shifted his consideration to the role of energy in economic structures. He reviewed the focus on monetary movements in economics, claiming that "real" wealth was obtained from the operation of energy to convert materials into physical goods and services. Soddy's economic articles were generally rejected in his time, but would slowly be applied to the development of bioeconomics and biophysical economics and also ecological economics in the late 20th century. Access to abundant, impartial information Post-scarcity civilizations have substantial access to impartial information and some design of education and life experience. Do we actually have the resources for this kind of society? Civilisation boils down to four components which are Raw Material, Energy, Information and human or artificial Intelligence none of which are in limited supply. It is the prevailing ineffective methods of handling and anticipated economic constraints that make it appear that there are significant limitations to these resources.

Frederick Soddy and Peter. H. Diamonds specifically pointed out that by using currently existing technology, the world should be able sustain it's populations no matter how larger the population increases by:

- We can provide abundant clean water for everyone on Earth
- We can produce enough food to feed at least 80 billion people without harming the environment
- We can meet our energy needs at least ten times over using clean, renewable energy
- We can build cheap, high-quality houses in a day or two, providing shelter for the billion people currently living in slums
- We can build technology of any complexity from free open-source designs and digitally fabricate them for the price of raw materials. And these raw materials are themselves extremely abundant. With every year that goes by, the methods of fabrication become more decentralized and the open-source designs become better, making this a more attractive option
- We can spread cheap, mobileInternet access to everyone on Earth, allowing them to connect to the world's informational and educational resources.
- Through open collaboration, this can network vast amounts of human intelligence, which can greatly accelerate scientific and technological progress
- We can make free educational materials available on the Internet, providing free education of unprecedented quality to everyone on Earth
- We can organize the World's medical knowledge, so that people have access to the highest-quality medical information and advice at all times

How do we establish a social framework advanced enough to provide for all of this? Looking at open collaborative designs and expectations. The inadequacy of Capital injection to the community can enforce limits upon societies that are conducive to material advancement. The demand for payment for subsistence motivates the desire for employment especially if there are no Government Subsidies for the population. Capital renders finite operative circulation within every community which inturn ensures abundance, recreation, enjoyment, and enhances their development. Capital injection is a prerequisite for business as consumers will have money to spend on goods. Capital enacted properly can avoid scarcity and will culminate in an abundant life for all. Europeans have instilled competitiveness through their education systems in place. Europeans have honoured competitiveness to the point of abursity. Their separateness psychology is developed from an early age i.e school test's and sport contesting. Our current Political Organizations worldwide organised around separateness instead of associations. The current losers and winners deprive the community from the collaborative and constructive input from the losers. True People Participative Governance should become the new Political Framework for all Democratic Governments. With the current mobile technologies in-place right now that can allow every voting individual the ability to vote on every Governmental Legislation that is passed through Parliament. It's time that the People's Voice/Vote be heard loud and clear in every Parliament in the World. This Current format of Member of Parliaments MP's representation is outdated and needs to be rejuvenated.

"True happiness is to enjoy the present, without anxious dependence upon the future, not to amuse ourselves with either hopes and fears but to rest satisfied with what we have, which is sufficient, for he that so wants nothing"....by Seneca

How do we get from here to there?

Dr. Adrian Bowyer, explained how we get there in a sentence? We do this by increasing the amount and capacity of physical goods through automation via readily available open-source channels, until it makes no sense for anyone to rely on anything else. The development beyond our present systems to post-scarcity, due to social and political reasons, may nevertheless be tougher than actually producing the technologies required to uphold a technological post-scarcity. However some construct of genuine post-scarcity perhaps administered at the personal consumption level unless recognized at a society/regional level for greater projects where all people on Earth do not have to work for income, or any kind of exchange, and have an extremely significant requirement standard of living appears possible on the experience of it. The Earth's surface consists of quintillions of tonnes of appropriate materials; energy is unlimited solar, geothermal, nuclear and automation of everything significant including the fabrication of other automated systems is likely to be within humanity's competences. Open-source design and engineering would be the next level of development design.

Potential routes to transition to post-scarcity

Here are three methods of how, it might be possible to transition from our current economy to a post-scarcity there may be others of course:

1) Advanced digital fabrication and closed-loop operations on a local scale - think of a very advanced version of Open Source Ecology who are operating at a small farm-scale.

2) Let industry compete to zero-cost or infinitesimally small cost through automation. The companies could be helped along by employing some open-source systems in their operations and even contributing to OS projects to reduce their costs in non-core areas. With companies in all industries eventually doing this to help them compete, the non-core areas from each industry may eventually all overlap, joining together to provide a complete alternative open-source infrastructure.

3) Intentional reproduction of all key infrastructure, assemble and utilities to eventually produce a corresponding automated open-source economy by open-source advocates considerable as was worked out in the software world, producing C compilers, performing system kernels, graphical desktops, IDE and Key Applications. It received a period to get that all in place but eventually it turned to a performance where Linux could be an essential OS for planners and now it is completely adaptable for typical computer users after about 20 years.

Power, control and jobs

A prevailing assertion is that existing people / companies / systems wouldn't let it develop however it is altogether another design of competition. In the same sense, considering established companies around doesn't stop startup companies from setting up and producing either. Incumbents can certainly make situations complex, but they are improbable to be effective to avoid it developing generally. If it is open-source and free or lower cost than an economic alternative then the commercial manufacturers and distributors may have a complicated time competing if the goods or services from the open-source manufacturers are of a comparable or marginally lower quality. You could argue that open-source systems and organisations serving at cost and driving it towards zero during the conversion duration are perhaps the transcendent illustration of dynamic market economics at work.

Human progress since the enlightenment has been rapid and frequently disruptive to the supposed status-quo. This is yet very considerable the situation today, and immediate-future group-scale open-source devices and services are a continuance of this. The consumers will be receiving greater preference for less and less cost. How jobs will be altered nevertheless with advancing automation is another issue altogether. Open-source hardware is yet very promising, but a striking illustration in the physical rather than software world is the creation of an open-source RepRap Machine, where it and its derivatives now make up a majority stake of new FDM 3D printers, according to Dr. Adrian Bowyer, an academic at the University of Bath and founder of the project. Interestingly as the average person's earning potential perhaps goes down as automation develops, the more efficiently and cheaply people will be able to get goods and services from automated open-source systems, so it may adjust to a particular extent. One extrapolated end-point is that as people's earning potential gradually falls to zero over time, all significant product and service costs will also be leaning towards zero. Another rather pessimistic alternative scenario, is that as automation advances, fewer and fewer people are able to afford the products produced by the prominent companies. This sounds improbable as commercial systems wouldn't be able to sustain if there were exceptionally few consumers in that market, so they might as easily end up giving things away by the time all significant production is executed 100% by machine, because what does it signify if all the companies costs were seeking the same direction too? However if the companies undertook not to do that, it wouldn't affect anyhow as the open-source providers would accept their place. This suggests to be unavoidable barring some kind of legal intervention. None of this would take place overnight so society would have improved, as it invariably has produced. This is why we nevertheless don't live in the stone-age.

"Post Scarcity" is essentially a utopian goal of economists. It means everything is free because natural resources are not privately owned and are no longer purposely made scarce. Matter of fact the entire study of economics would be redundant in a world where resources were unlimitedly unlimited and not scarce. But to actually immerse your intellect around the conception of "post scarcity" you have to consider what it undoubtedly means. If resources were boundless, everything would be free. Automobiles would be free just as gumballs would be free. And because everything is free, then NOTHING would have value. There would be no prices. Just "stuff." You can kind of imagine this if you've ever watched Star Trek Movies where they have the replicator. As a youth you might reply, "Well I'd replicate diamonds and be rich!" But the dilemma is there is no "rich" or "poor" in a post-scarcity economy. The diamonds have no value because they can be reproduced ad-infinitum, just like everything else. Again, NOTHING would have value, NOTHING would have a cost matter of fact in a genuinely 100% post scarcity economy, you wouldn't indeed have money.

Inalienable human rights are permanent, no matter if most of human history appeared not to adhere to it. It might be that the events that constitute economic productivity have matched a position in developing the expectations of human populations, but that shows no role in it being wrong. One could state this against any possible assessment of the present system. 'Well, your philosophy isn't as economically productive as history would demand it to be.' It means nothing, but let's recognize it anyhow. By that philosophy what we have at all moments is something that is or strives to be the most economically expedient ideology, but why would these forces suggest at all moments efficiency over other valuable elements? Efficiency itself can only be valuable inasmuch as it can lead to other valuable things. Efficiency can't be an independent value; On its own it is nothing. Imagine a future society in which all intense human labour is supplanted by machines. What would be money and employment if all the work is completed by machines with no operating human labour input? In an entirely automated society money has essentially no purpose, due to its high efficiency and employment by humans wouldn't exist. Would the owners of such machines self sustain or not give such non owners freely? There is no work, so how could non-owners of such machines gain any goods/services? What restrains us currently from reaching that kind of a society?

Dr. Adrian Bowyer,went on to state "My objective is that there are at least two possible complications in maintaining a society in which everything is entirely automated. The initial one is clearly technology itself, but the more significant reason since it could invalidate the original one is the interest of the rentier class to survive in power, which ends up in a perpetual inclination to obstruct the emancipatory potential of machines. Make more service jobs, higher the request for goods artificially etc. There are many ways of vindicating the dissemination of money, when technology becomes more efficient. One can't look at new technology in a vacuum and presume it would lead to anything by itself, it is regularly interconnected with the economic network".

A popular rally cry of the labour movements was "needs over profit." There was ofcourse a response to it. "Well, the reason for the theory that capitalism encourages human benefit is pretty familiar. It works something like this: Capitalist organizations exist only if they make money and they make money only if they succeed in competition against other capitalist enterprises. Since that competition is severe, the firm to survive has to be efficient. If firms produce incompetently, they go under. So, they have to seize every opportunity to enhance their productive materials and capabilities so that they can produce cheaply enough, to make enough money, to go on. It's indicated in this rationalization of capitalism that the capitalist firm doesn't plan to satisfy people but the firm can't get what they are focusing at, which is money, unless they do satisfy people and satisfy them better than rival enterprises do. Well, I agree with part of this assertion; Capitalist competition, that has to be acknowledged, has engendered a remarkable expansion in our power to produce things, but the controversy also mentions that capitalism satisfies people and I'm going to challenge that the nature the system controls technological progress generates widespread frustration, not satisfaction.

Dr. Adrian Bowyer's anti-capitalist argument commenced with the absolute same proposal with which the argument praising capitalism begins namely this hypothesis that the purpose of the capitalist firm is to make as much money as possible. It isn't essentially concerned in serving anybody's needs. It measures its performance by how much profit it generates. Now that doesn't prove straight off that it isn't desirable at serving needs in fact the evidence for capitalism that I suggested a moment ago might be presented as follows: Competing firms trying not to satisfy needs but to make money will in fact make our needs extremely well since they can't make money unless they do so. Okay, that's the debate, but I'm now going to prove that the fact that capitalist enterprises aren't interested in serving human needs does have destructive repercussions. Recall that development in productivity is required if the firm is going to survive in competition. Now what does increased productivity mean? It means more gain for every component of Labor and that means that you can do two different things when productivity goes up. One system of using enhanced productivity is to shorten work and increase leisure, while performing the same profit as before. Alternatively output may be enhanced, while labor remains the same. Now let's grant that more productivity is a wonderful thing but it's also correct that for most people what they have to do to earn a living isn't a source of satisfaction. Most people's jobs after all are such that they serve not only from more goods and services but also from a shorter working day and longer holidays.

But the concern with the quest for goods in a capitalist society is that we'll repeatedly, most of us, require more Goods than we can get, since the capitalist system serves to assure that people's yearning for goods is never fulfilled. Institutions of course prefer content consumers, but they mustn't become extremely content, since when consumers are content with what they've had, they buy less and work less and business diminishes.

"That's why in a capitalist society a colossal amount of creation and capability goes into trying to get people to want what they don't have. It can't achieve the probabilities of emancipation it creates having reversed the hindrance of natural scarcity it manipulates an artificial scarcity which means that people never feel they have enough. Capitalism moves humanity to the extreme verge of emancipation and then bolts the gate; We get near it, but we persist on a treadmill just outside it."...By G. A Cohen Please do watch his speech on youtube G. A Cohen speech against Capitalism. Many companies of non-employment already survived. If you suggest it is only theoretically impossible not empirically then it has no normative importance to recommending such a capitalistic system. Further, this would also violate Ostrom's law "A resource arrangement that functions in work can work in theory." such as in 1936 Spain will be the most natural case here. One can just position to different systems that did occur, that are in consonance with that information. So a particular system could have an identical system as the ones that are brought up, with diversity to the intensity that it remains possible. Unless, you want to express that it did exist and is by now inconceivable, because of factual occurrences that can't remain any longer. However, this is yet something open that needs to be questioned.

To make such a case one would desire to demonstrate that it is possible to have events that are actually dependent on time alone. Last but not least, don't compare my stand to people who support China has become paperless. I shall state an assumption which I will call definatory consent. If, let's say, two people want to have a debate with normative significance and both have an extraordinary position on a subject, then each position has to agree to each other's own interpretation of their own position. Unless one view can demonstrate that the other position has a problem within the interpretation that both sides know what word refers to their position and that the definition always is in accordance with the position that the mentioned side holds. (It's not important what word they use to refer to a position. It is important that both sides know what they are arguing about while knowing each other's position. "Capitalism can hardly be criticized for not vanquishing ideas that haven't meaningfully come into being." Now you have got the time to rethink this. Naturally, a 100% post-scarcity world is actually impossible. Even if we perfect 3 d printing, you need people to maintain the 3d printers, people to transport goods, electricity, not to mention maintain the infrastructure of society as well as some government services to manage the humans. But what is interesting about economics and humanity is that though a 100% pure post-scarcity economy is impossible, we are constantly, asymptotically approaching it. Just 100 years ago food was kind of a huge issue. Now it isn't. Just 250 year ago, electricity was a huge non-existent issue. Now it isn't. And thus, though we will never have EVERYTHING be truly free, because of technological advances, we are constantly closing in on that post scarcity goal.

This then leads the human mind into an interesting world. If 3d printers actually deliver on all of their promises, it will be the first time in human history where your physical needs are met at zero or near zero cost. This then behooves the question "What will humans do or pursue in life?" Realize you, me and everybody else works a fair percentage of our lives working up the money to pay for everything. But if "everything" or most everything were free, what would the economy be about then? What would humans work and live for? The answer is other humans. Specifically, sex and attention. Imagine again there is no such thing as money. Material goods and physical possessions are limitlessly abundant. What would then have any kind of value in this society and economy? Well, with physical goods being completely free, the only thing would be non-physical goods or services, namely provided by humans. And because of our binary sexual nature, this would leave only two goods or services left to be traded. Sex and recognition. Men would want sex from women and women would want attention from men. Of course, this industry has consistently been going on, but has been frustrated or perplexed with physical goods. Men desired to demonstrate their income earning potential to persuade women that they are suitable providers, so they would buy "expensive things" like sports cars. But all this in a post-scarcity world, this role would be rendered obsolete, dismissing the man solely to his capability to provide attention to connect some sex. Women would also encounter a considerable more simplified economy. Instead of having to work all those extra hours to buy a prada purse and pay off her debts, she now just has to earn mens' attention by solely fixating on her physical beauty. And this is where it turns scary.

Digital currencies can be the bridge to narrow the disparity between the wealthy and the poor in an instant performance of making everybody a millionaire overnight. The evolution of the internet has changed the world economy. Globalisation of markets has become much easier, in fact it has presented a new medium for marketers to offer their products and services. The Digital report for 2018 Showed that half the world is online amounting to 4,021 billion people. Much of the sudden growth in internet users is driven by the availability of smartphones. Users in SubAfrica comprise a total count of 420 million mobile users with a 43% penetration rate for Digital Marketers. By 2025 Africa had been predicted to have a half a billion internet users making Africa the fastest growing mobile market. According to the report there were 731 million Sim connections in Africa in 2018, it's expected to rise to 1 billion by 2020. Smartphone connections have doubled in Sub-Saharan Africa over the past 5 years to over 500 million users. Digital Report, (2018) According to Tiago and Verissimo (2014) "Human interactions have changed significantly due to engagement on social networks: their rapid growth of the web platforms has facilitated behavioural changes related to activities, habitats, and interaction. Open your perspectives. The Universe is vast. It's fascinating to be born at this time because we have to adjust everything for the better for humanity and not just for a few European Aristocracies. Wake Up World time think and reexamine our lives and why we are working and for what purpose? Why are we chasing paper money to live?.

Once Stalin turned to one meeting with a living chicken. He commenced to pluck its feathers one by one off. The chicken quacked in deep agony, blood oozing from its pores. It gave out heartbreaking cries but a Satlin continued without remorse plucking feather after feather until the chicken was utterly naked. After that, he flung the chicken on the ground and from his pockets, took out some chicken feed and started to throw it at the poor chicken. It started eating and as he strode away the chicken followed him and sat at his feet feeding from his palm. Satlin then told members of his party "This chicken represents the people, you must disempower them , brutalize them, beat them up and leave them. If you do this and then give them peanuts when they are in a helpless and desperate situation, they will blindly follow you for the rest of their life. They will think you are a hero forever. They will forget that, it is you who brought them to the situation in the first place" Now people, doesn't this sound familiar? To the Capitalistic life we are living now time to wake up from the capitalist's deceptions.

I hope mankind can recreate a different life from what we know it now where everyone's a millionaire with unlimited access to funds. Mankind should aim to create a world where everyone lives in abundance and never needs for anything but to try to find themselves. We should all aim to recreate life from what we have now, economics shouldn't be the aim for humans but living life. Capitalism is certainly an unhuman concept and we have to eradicate it ASAP!!! Heaven on earth is what we need for every human living in Abundance like the 1% European Elite at the moment my dream is by introducing a Global Digital currency is the best way to go about it and issue everyone with equal amounts of wealth for the World as nearly everyone has a digital mobile phone, and it will work wonders in Countries like Zimbabwe and The DRC. East African MTN Epesa Digital banking and transactions is uplifting the Eastern African Community. China is now paperless and all transactions are digital. Countries are looking at issuing their own digital currencies for several reasons, experts say. One is to counter the rise of new cryptocurrencies payment methods outside the country's control, such as Bitcoin. Some countries that are exploring national digital currencies, including China, have simultaneously restricted the creation and trading of other cryptocurrencies. National digital currencies could have a wide range of advantages and implications. If a national digital currency were issued by the central bank and were exchangeable with paper money, its value would be more stable as a payment method than cryptocurrencies like Bitcoin, experts say. Some suggest that introducing a digital currency would help speed the shift toward a cashless society; it would reduce cost and boost productivity, because businesses and individuals wouldn't have to manage cash or pay charges such as ATM fees. In addition, some experts suggest that if central banks issue accounts directly to individuals and shareholders, the move could reduce the need for retail banks.

Experts also suggest that a nationwide digital currency could help combat tax dodge and illegitimate economic enterprise. Replacing cash with digital money could also make it clearer for central banks to lower interest rates below zero per cent, when needed, because "shareholders would have no currency to rush to," corresponding to one authority. In developing economies, digital currencies could increase financial involvement by making a digital payment method available to many more people. As cryptocurrencies such as Bitcoin have taken off worldwide, countries great and small are vigorously researching the possibility of issuing their own national digital currencies. Central banks in significant economies, including the U.S. and China, are investigating the potential benefits, deficiencies, and systems. However, only a handful of poorer countries have issued their own digital currencies to date and some of those payment methods are restricted in scope. MTN Africa Epesa Digital payments is making trends in Africa.

There is a considerable compromise of controversy on the elementals of how governmental digital currencies would work, as well as the benefits they might provide as a payment method. Experts point out that indeed today, currency remains predominantly in digital appearing as it is issued, mortgaged, and used in payments by central and private banks. A key characteristic is that a governmental digital currency does not have a tangible cash form such as banknotes or coins, although it could be switched to physical currency and vice versa. In a journal published in 2017 by the Hoover Institution think tank, economists considered two possible ways that a governmental digital currency could work. One proposal, which they regarded analogous to physical cash, would be for an Central Bank to issue currency as digital tokens, which would then circulate as a payment method among industries and individuals and might only infrequently be redeposited back at the Central Bank. This approach would use a blockchain to verify and track transactions. In another approach, analogous to debit cards, businesses and individuals would hold accounts directly at the Central Bank or at their managed financial institutions.

The payment method would be the central bank debiting the payer's account and crediting the payee's account. This differs from the present system, as administered in countries such as the U.S. and U.K., in which the central bank operates accounts for other financial institutions but not for individuals. As the Bank of England points out: "At the moment, we provide electronic accounts to banks and key financial institutions, but the public can only hold central bank money in physical form as banknotes. If a central bank were to issue a digital currency everyone, including businesses, households and financial institutions other than banks could store value and make payments in electronic central bank money in addition to being able to pay with cash. While this may seem like a small change, it could have wide-ranging implications for monetary policy and financial stability."

Countries are looking at issuing their own digital currencies for several reasons, experts say. One is to counter the rise of new cryptocurrencies payment methods outside the country's control, such as Bitcoin. Some countries that are exploring national digital currencies, including China, have simultaneously restricted the creation and trading of other cryptocurrencies. National digital currencies could have a wide range of advantages and implications. If a national digital currency were issued by the central bank and were exchangeable with paper money, its value would be more stable as a payment method than cryptocurrencies like Bitcoin, experts say. Some suggest that introducing a digital currency would help speed the shift toward a cashless society; it would reduce cost and boost productivity, because businesses and individuals wouldn't have to manage cash or pay charges such as ATM fees. In addition, some experts suggest that if central banks issue accounts directly to individuals and shareholders, the move could reduce the need for retail banks.

Estonia is proposing to establish a cryptocurrency with the working name "estcoin," according to a blog post by the director of the country's advanced "e-residency" digital initiative. However, estcoin could not become the representative governmental digital currency, since Estonia is part of the EU and uses the euro as its currency, affirming the blog post. Instead, the country is considering several variations of estcoin, which might be accepted to verify existence in blockchain-based transactions, or as a payment method that is exchangeable with euros. Bank commissioners in many of the World's Biggest Economies have suggested they are researching national digital currencies even though most have also announced they have no firm program or timetable for introducing such a system of payment. They comprise the U.S., as several Federal Reserve officials announced in 2017.

"It's certainly premature to be speaking about the Reserve banks offering digital currencies, but it is something we are considering," stated New York Federal Reserve President William Dudley, according to the Wall Street Journal. Other officials suggested that a cautious approach is needed, noting considerations such as the potential for cyberattacks. China's central bank has gone digital currency and has indeed created and tested a prototype, according to reports. China is the world leader in mobile payment volume, and a digital currency could give the Chinese government better surveillance over billions of digital transactions, while diminishing activity costs. According to experts, this could increase financial involvement and help undermine corruption. "Virtual currency is easier to track, allowing the central bank to track its velocity and the whereabouts of the money and improve its monetary policies accordingly," according to the official heading exploration into the currency at the central bank.

The Bank of England has been investigating the possibility of introducing its own digital currency since 2015, but expresses it has no present proposals to do so. One article suggested this is due at least in part to considerations about the impact on conventional banks and the larger financial system. The Bank anticipated that consumers would prefer to have an account at the central bank rather than at a retail bank, and was concerned about the potential financial confusion. In Japan, a consortium of banks aims to launch a digital currency in time for the 2020 Tokyo Olympics, which has sadly been postponed due to the CoronaVirus. With responsibilities from each country's central bank, according to the Financial Times. One goal of the effort is reportedly to respond to competition from major mobile-payment services from Chinese and U.S. corporations. The so-called "J-Coin" would be convertible with the Japanese yen on a one-to-one basis. In return for providing the service for free, the banks would benefit by collecting more data on consumer spending sequences, the Financial Times announced. Other countries that are researching the possibility of a nationwide digital currency consist of Canada, Australia, Sweden, Israel, and Russia.

This isn't to say what is proposed here may happen, but that it could happen it is feasible from a physical and technological viewpoint today. It is a matter of spreading the knowledge that these things are possible and enough people choosing to work towards it. African Governments should favour the planning and the setting up non-market allocation of financial resources through a variety of controls and government incentives for prices for domestic and foriegn trade structures as proposed by Professor Maitreesh Ghatak in his 2015 World Bank Report. People will not have to suffer drudgery and what amounts to wage slavery during the best years of their lives. Unfortunately a large proportion of people today in both white and blue collar jobs would really rather be doing something else than the jobs they are employed to do. They feel perhaps that what they are doing is not directly relevant to their lives or is not particularly interesting and feel they are simply a cog with little control in a larger machine. Currently they have to do it to afford food, shelter and goods. A post-scarcity society enables them to have the time and space to work on things that are important to them, and to learn the skills needed to reach their goals and have room to be more creative.

This isn't to say what is proposed here may happen, but that it could happen as it is feasible from a physical and technological viewpoint today...By Vincent Happy Mnisi

The Population and Environmental Factors

The Population element will perform a significant role as we all will desire to establish a world of divine contentment and total wealth for everybody on earth. People Participative Governance (PPG) should form the next democratic framework, allowing every citizen the ability to vote on parliamentary decisions, this can be accomplished utilising our current mobile technologies in applications (APPS). The current party politics concept is flawed. MP's and Prime Ministers shouldn't be party led but they should be able to exercise their own personal concise and personal decision instead of being forced to vote the party line. The army concept is crazy training human beings to slaughter each other, the desire for defence allocations in this day and age is obsolete as the demand to overthrow and dominate should be done away with by now. A display of power is a presentation of weakness and humans shouldn't be building up nuclear ammunition because it will kill the world. There is widespread concern about an 'overpopulation complication'. Let us be clear about what is meant by 'overpopulation'. It is not a problem for a lot of people to be awake? It is a problem if there are too many people for given resources to go around. So the essential investigation is, "Is the human population likely to outstrip available resources?" In demographics, the world population is the total estimate of humans presently living, and has reached 7.7 billion people as of 1st April 2020. This number is growing; the UN's upper prediction is 10.6 billion for 2050. After that, the UN forecasts the population to begin to fall. Let us embrace that the population proceeds to swell beyond 2050 and approaches 40 billion, Would we be overpopulated then, in relation to available resources? Food. 35 million babies have been born in the past three months worldwide and 15 million deaths.

The sacristy model dates back to the late eighteenth century when British Scholar Thomas Robert Malthus realised that while food production expanded linearly populations grow exponentially. Malths was quite certain that they would come at a time where we would exceed our capacity to feed ourselves. He once stated "The power of the population is indefinetely greater than the power of the earth to produce subsistence for man" Sadly his concerns were echoed by Dr Martin Luther King Jr who stated "Unlike the plagues of the dark ages or contemporary diseases which we don't understand, the modern plague of the overpopulation is soluble by means we have discovered and with resources we poses". Dr Pauk Ehrlich a Biologist from Stanford University further amplified it with his publication of *"The Population Bomb"*. In 1968 Industrialist Aurelio Peccei organised a gathering of Multidisciplinary groups of international thinkers to a meeting now known as the Club of Rome. At this meeting they discussed the problems of short-term thinking in a long-term world. In 1972 they published their results from their discussions ``*The limits to growth"* it instantly became a classic bestseller selling over 12 million copies in thirty languages and scaring everyone who read it. In this publication The Club of Rome compared worldwide population growth to global resource consumption rates in effect stating in this book that the world was running out of resources and we are running out of time too.

Our world has about 1260 quintillion liters of water. This means that 40 billion people using 200 liters a day each would help, over the course of a year, less than 0.00025% of the world's water. The world used 15 terawatts of energy in 2008. If rising population and increasing technology increased this 100-fold to 1500 terawatts, we would still only need to convert less than 0.9% of the sunlight that falls on Earth. It is extremely likely that we will have fusion reactors and space-based solar panels before our energy needs come anywhere near this achievement. The world's surface including oceans is about 510 million square kilometers. According to Atlas World, one-eighth of this, 63,750,000km2, is habitable land. For a population of 40 billion people, this is 1593.75m2 habitable land per person, equivalent to an average population density of 628 people per km2. This is proportional to a fairly densely populated. Without expanding farmland, we could produce enough food for 80 billion people employing low-tech permaculture systems only. Our world has about 1260 quintillion liters of water. This means that 40 billion people using 200 liters a day each would help, over the course of a year, less than 0.00025% of the world's water. 100 years ago, 8000 square meters of land was needed to grow food for an individual. It can now be performed on a few hundred square meters. Why? Because Human intellect has figured out how to extract more resources from a limited amount of material. The achievement of human perception is constantly to enable us to achieve more for less, better solar cells can make more electricity from less sunlight, we can make a more vigorous computer chip using less material than a few generations ago, and more efficient electric automobiles can travel the same journeys with much less petrol.

With the expectation of massive technological advances in the coming decades, a scenario often crops up that some see as an unlikely wildcard, and others see as an inevitable evolution of current trends: that of a post-scarcity society, in which technology has accorded all people access to the necessary resources and opportunities to live decent and dignified lives. Even though the most likely scenario for society and education 50 years from now may be one that still resembles our current model though the exact nature of this model may change profoundly, a post-scarcity scenario is realistic enough to be worth discussing. Better access to basic necessities could lead to a fundamental shift in the nature and purpose of education, with education increasingly becoming a quest for meaning and fulfilment rather than being a prerequisite for labour market participation. A post-scarcity society is one where every inhabitant can certainly afford all the necessities of life. Massive labour market automation and quantity of cheap energy and raw materials thanks to technological advances make products and services basically free. It's a society of abundance. Human Intellect is the key that unlocks all other resources. As Robert Anton Wilson has stated, "You can starve in the middle of a field of wheat if your mind hasn't identified wheat as edible." The vaster the population, the grander the stockpile of human intelligence.

Senior Futurist, Editor for Copenhagen Institute for future studies KLAUS Æ. MOGENSEN in an article on education in a post-scarcity society pointed out that a substantial population that is well structured and edcutaded will concoct and communicate all kinds of technological solutions that enable us to do more with the resources we have. And so, paradoxically, an enlarged population can mean that we have more resources to go around Some 'luxury' products and services may still be scarce and therefore more problematic to secure, and there may also be powerful economic polarisation in a post-scarcity society, but no one lacks anything fundamental to their well-being, and everybody has access to most opportunities through a global basic income and/or a comprehensive basic assets system that consists of free food, sheltering, media, education, public transport, and other essential needs. A post-scarcity society is not automatically a sustainable society. It may be financed by forwarding the bill to future generations, for example by ignoring unsustainable resource and energy usage and long-term climate change; but it is fairly possible to imagine a sustainable post scarcity economy.

To make a post-scarcity society possible, several advances will be required:

- The manufacture of products and provision of services must be mostly automated and based on raw materials that are plentiful or recyclable
- Energy must be cheap and preferably sustainable, e.g. based on renewable resources.
- The alarming threat of climate change and the consequences associated with it need to be managed/mitigated
- Artificial Intelligence must be advanced enough to handle the basic cognitive tasks necessary to keep an advanced society running, including the administration and operation of infrastructure, healthcare, transport, and education
- People aren't required to work to justify their existence. However, post-scarcity does not mean post-work, as the quest for personal fulfilment might still compel many to work
- The benefits of the above advances are made available to all. While some may have access to far more wealth and opportunities than others, no one lacks anything essential.

While we are moderately near a post-scarcity society today, none of the advances noted above suggest unsurmountable over a timeframe of five decades. Robots and technology such as preservative manufacturing (3D-printing) are making their entry into an expanding number of industries, and AI is becoming capable of operating tasks previously demanding exceptionally skilled human labour. The World Economic Forum even anticipated that machines will be doing 52 per cent of work tasks by 2025 compared to 29 per cent today reducing human labour needs by a third in just 7 years as anticipated by Dr. Adrian Bowyer,

At the same time, the costs of solar power, wind power and lithium-ion battery storage have declined significantly in recent years, and there is slight evidence to suggest that the price of energy will not continue to decline in the future as modern energy technologies continue to improve and new solutions emerge. The greatest drawbacks to the development of a post-scarcity society may well be political and cultural rather than pragmatic and technological. We will have a society where most people don't work, but still derive an income worthy of being at work? Will we observe increasing economic polarisation due to the development of a 'winner-takes all' economy, despite comprehensive basic income? Will individuals still want to work out of a desire for fulfilment, even though their livelihoods won't depend on it? Challenges like these will shape both the nature and purpose of higher education in a post scarcity society.(Elden, 1981)

Post-scarcity education

Gratuitous to say, higher education in a post-scarcity society will look remarkably different from what it is today. Technology will play a major role in increasing capacity, access and quality of education across the world. The degree of automation and digitisation of education in a post-scarcity society means that it costs extraordinarily meager to provide a universal essential education to all. Equally essential is the fact that most people pursue an essential level of formalised higher education, which is freely available to all on the internet. Formalised basic level higher education is predominantly a governmental affair, but besides that, the education market will need to be ultimately globalised.

Individuals should be able to freely join completely individualised online educational experiences powered by Artificial Intelligence (AI), which will draw into history the individuals' personal interests, aspirations, weaknesses, cultural backgrounds, etc. AI-guided automated translation has eliminated most language restraints, but cultural ones persist. However, not all aspects of higher education can be ultimately automated, and conventional face-to-face learning has become a premium luxury only available to a select few. For example, students who have shown extraordinary genius and commitment in online courses and virtual workshops may be invited to physical elite research institutions for further specialised, supervised education and real experimental science and innovation.(Dr. Adrian Bowyer,2020)

While everybody will have access to some level of formalised higher education, informal and self-trained learning has generally come to the vanguard. Especially lifelong learning takes place in a flexible and informal environment. With the significant level of connectivity in society, essentially simulated learning environments provide interactive and immersive learning experiences in virtually all aspects of life, whether it is through virtual experimental workshops, true-to-life interactive tours to significant sites or unusual atmospheres, or something else entirely. Neuroscientists have formed a system to amplify learning using brain-computer interfaces, and as a potential game changer, they assert they are not significant from new major improvements that could make it possible to feed knowledge directly into people's brains to instruct new skills in an instant. We have totally begun a 'ubiquitous learning' paradigm and anytime, anywhere learning environment reinforced by technology. This 5G technology being installed in 2020 will permit for direct downloading to the brain.

The purpose of education in a post-scarcity society

In an abundant post-scarcity scenario, Artificial Intelligence (AI) will handle many of the tasks that are intrinsic to fields such as law, economics, medicine, architecture, engineering, education, and design. However, eminently skilled specialists are still needed to provide knowledge and science, though even here, AI plays a grander role, for example in running virtual analysis situations. As artificial intelligence and automation have taken over most conventional jobs, people are generally no longer pursuing education to be able to compete in work markets. With participation in the labour market no longer being the main motivation to pursue higher education, the role of higher education institutions will be altered fundamentally. Overall, there is less demand for formalised university education, and universities have reverted to their previous role as institutions devoted to advanced research. Citizens of the post-scarcity society prefer to pursue higher education in different frameworks for diverse reasons, but mainly in an attempt to live a purposeful life. After all, even in a society where material needs have been generally eradicated, humans will likely still seek the satisfaction that develops from learning new things or achieving new skills, and for many people, the quest for personal fulfilment still urges them to carry out work they find worthwhile. Citizens of the post-scarcity society are encouraged to pursue higher education with the aim of learning essential life skills, skills one needs to make the most out of life. (Dr. Adrian Bowyer,2020)

Future literacy has emerged as a significant life experience for individuals to better recognize the role the future plays in the present, and to nurture the competence to respond and adapt effectively to evolving circumstances. Climate literacy skills remain essential in the continuing battle to address the repercussions of global climate change. Interest in past times, when individual ability mattered more, has grown. History, including counterfactual history, has become a popular pastime and field of education. Fields like philosophy and psychology have also seen a renaissance in a world where living is easy but finding the meaning of life is hard. Population growth, if it continues long enough, may also lead to unavoidable scarcity. As pointed out by Paul Ehrlich, Albert Bartlett, and others, exponential growth in the human population has the capacity to overwhelm any finite supply of resources, even the entire known universe, in a remarkably short time. For example, if the human population could continue to grow indefinitely at its 1994 rate, in 1,900 years the mass of the human population would equal the mass of Earth, and in 6000 years the mass of the human population would equal the estimated mass of the observable universe. Although this would imply the invention of faster than light travel, necessary for humanity to spread throughout the universe as fast as population growth, even at lower growth rates these levels would still be reached in readily imaginable times.

It is accordingly problematic to develop a reliable post scarcity scenario which does not also involve zero population growth or extremely low population growth. Population in the world is presently (2020) growing at an estimate of around 1.05% per year down from 1.08% in 2019, 1.10% in 2018, and 1.12% in 2017. The present average population increase is estimated at 81 million people per year. Annual growth rate reached its peak in the late 1960s, when it was at around 2%. The rate of increase has virtually halved since then, and will continue to decline in the coming years. World population will accordingly continue to flourish in the 21st century, but at a considerable slower rate compared to the recent past. World population has doubled (100% increase) in 40 years from 1959 (3 billion) to 1999 (6 billion). It is now estimated that it will take another approximately 40 years to increase by another 50% to become 9 billion by 2037. The latest world population projections reveal that world population will approach 10 billion individuals in the year 2057.

World Population (2020 and historical)

Advocates also frequently argue that the energy and raw materials available could be enormously expanded if we considered resources beyond the Earth. For example, asteroid mining is frequently considered as an alternative of enormously diminishing scarcity for many practical minerals such as nickel, tin, gold etc. While early asteroid mining might involve manned missions, advocates hope that eventually humanity could have automated mining conducted by self-replicating machines. If this were undertaken, then the only capital expenditure would be a single self-replicating unit (whether robotic or nanotechnological), after which the number of units could replicate at no further cost, limited only by the available raw materials needed to develop more.(D.Masley.2017)

It was written during the 1970s by The UN that 75% of the people who had ever been born were alive at that moment. This was grossly false. Assuming that we start counting from about 50,000 B.C., the time when modern Homo sapiens appeared on the earth (and not from 700,000 B.C. when the ancestors of Homo sapiens appeared, or several million years ago when hominids were present), taking into account that all population data are a rough estimate, and assuming a constant growth rate applied to each period up to modern times, it has been estimated that a total of approximately **106 billion people** have been born since the dawn of the human species, making the population currently alive roughly 6% of all people who have ever lived on planet Earth. Others have estimated the number of human beings who have ever lived to be anywhere from 45 billion to 125 billion, with most estimates falling into the range of **90 to 110 billion** humans.

Previous Milestones

- **7 Billion: 2019**
- **6 Billion: 2010**
- **5 Billion: 1987**
- **4 Billion: 1974**
- **3 Billion: 1960**
- **2 Billion: 1930**
- **1 Billion: 1804**

World Population by Religion

According to a study done in the 2010 world population of 6.9 billion by The Pew Forum, there are:

- **2,173,180,000 Christians (31%** of world population), of which 50% are Catholic, 37% Protestant, 12% Orthodox, and 1% other.
- **1,598,510,000 Muslims (23%)**, of which 87-90% are Sunnis, 10-13% Shia.
- **1,126,500,000 No Religion affiliation (16%)**: atheists, agnostics and people who do not identify with any particular religion. One-in-five people (20%) in the United States are religiously unaffiliated.
- **1,033,080,000 Hindus (15%)**, the overwhelming majority (94%) of which live in India.
- **487,540,000 Buddhists (7%)**, of which half live in China.
- **405,120,000 Folk Religionists (6%)**: faiths that are closely associated with a particular group of people, ethnicity or tribe.
- **58,110,000 Other Religions (1%)**: Baha'i faith, Taoism, Jainism, Shintoism, Sikhism, Tenrikyo, Wicca, Zoroastrianism and many others.
- **13,850,000 Jews (0.2%)**, four-fifths of which live in two countries: United States (41%) and Israel (41%).

World Population clock: sources and methodology

The world population counter displayed on Worldometer takes into consideration data from two major sources: the United Nations and every country's populations census.

1. The United Nations Population Division of the Department of Economic and Social Affairs every two years calculates, updates, and publishes estimates of total population in its World Population Prospects series. These population estimates and projections provide the standard and consistent collection of population figures that are used throughout the United Nations System.

   The World Population as from April 2020 presents the most recent data available (issued in April of 2020). Estimates and predicted world population and country specific populations are given from 1950 through 2100 and are released every two years. Worldometer, as it is a common process, applies the medium fertility estimates. Data underlying the population estimates are governmental and sub national census data and data on births, deaths, and immigrants available from national sources and publications, as well as from surveys. For all countries, census and registration data are assessed and, if necessary, improved for deficiency by the Population Division as part of its measures of the official United Nations population estimates and projections.

2. Finally, since most recent data for a single country is often at least two years old, the current world population figure is necessarily a projection of past data based on assumed trends. As new data become available, assumptions and data are reevaluated and past conclusions and current figures may be modified. For information about how these estimates and projections are made by the U.S. Census Bureau, see the Population Estimates and Projections Methodology.

Current World Population

7,775,112,400

view all people on 1 page >

Today

Births today

338,874

Deaths today

142,267

Population Growth today

196,607

This year

Births this year

35,632,247

Deaths this year

14,959,270

Population Growth this year

The above world population clock is based on the latest estimates released on 2nd of April 2020 at 9.13 pm by the United Nations Worldometer which is a particular website that shows live counters that are based on U.N. data.

Predicting changes in the redistribution of food and the abundance of prosperity for the entire world population. Environmental changes are expected to develop both the distribution and the abundance of structures. An unreasonable volume of previous work has concentrated on distribution alone, either documenting historical range shifts or anticipating future occurrence sequences. However, simultaneous predictions of abundance and distribution across landscapes would be far more useful. To critically evaluate which concepts represent advances towards the objective of joint predictions of profusion and distribution, we review recent work on changing distributions and on effects of environmental drivers on specific populations. Several systems have been used to anticipate changing distributions. Some of these can be efficiently customized to also predict abundance, but others cannot. In parallel, demographers have developed a much stronger grasp of how changing abiotic and biotic drivers will determine growth rate and abundance in particular populations. However, this demographic work has seldom accepted a landscape perspective and has generally neglected the effects of intraspecific density. I encourage a synthetic procedure in which population models accounting for both density dependence and effects of environmental drivers are used to create integrated predictions of equilibrium abundance and distribution across entire landscapes. Such predictions would establish a significant step forward in estimating the ecological effects of environmental changes.(Elden, 1981)

Change can happen consciously or subconsciously, I am certain that each of us have at least experienced some sort of imagination on the qualities we seek in existence in one form or another. However, seizing control in visualisation might not ultimately realise in many and here I am, emphasizing that we can naturally influence our subconscious mind to naturally attract what we seek in life to us. Our brain cannot differentiate physical and synthetic memories/imagination those that are vividly imagined, and when imagined enough with striking illustrations, our subconscious will consider that we have previously accomplished it and provide us the resources we need to succeed. A significant clue is that the brain doesn't choose sides. If you continually feed it with dreadful images, of replaying failures and generate emotions of misery and anxiety, bad experiences will occur for everyone it's part of life. Simple law of attraction applies, likewise, if we feed our brain with rich, motivating and inspiring imaginations, positive association will result with these dreams and appropriate emotions, then giving fulfilling, life altering experiences. Do note before you go on to creative visualisations. Visualise the desirable things. Remember that your brain does not choose sides. Set goals before visualising if you succeed, not keep your mind positively, it guides you instead. Set your personal values before progressing on to discovering your life purpose and coordinating to your visualisation. Be disciplined and committed, setting aside time each day to visualise for best results.(R. Byrne, 2006)

A significant pointer is that the brain doesn't pick up sides. If you continually feed it with bad images, of replaying failures and generate perceptions of uncertainty and anxiety, bad experiences will occur. Natural law of attraction applies, likewise, if we feed our brain with rich, motivating and inspiring imaginations, positive association will take place with these dreams and positive emotions, then allowing fulfilling, life altering experiences. Learn to write your thoughts down and afterwards work on them in creative visualisations of attainment. Visualise the desirable things! Remember that your brain does not take sides Set goals before visualising if you manage not direct your perceiving positively, it directs you instead. Set your personal values before going on to identifying life purpose and associating to visualisation. Be disciplined and committed, setting aside time each day to visualise for best results, there are however a number of distractions and choices that may develop in life, and therefore we cannot leave visualisation to chance. By instilling a discipline to visualise what we seek, provide coherent and sustaining successes, aligned to our life purpose.

Karl Marx, stated in a section of his Grundrisse that was to could recognized as the "Fragment on Machines", suggested that the development to a post-capitalist society incorporated with upgrades in automation would provide for considerable reductions in workforce required to manufacture necessary goods, ultimately arriving at a position where all communities would have substantial amounts of leisure time to engage in education, the arts, and creative endeavors; a state some critics previously characterized as "post-scarcity". Marx asserted that capitalism the dynamic of economic growth based on capital accumulation depends on exploiting the surplus labor of employees, but a post-capitalist society would allow for the independent development of individualities, and hence not the devaluation of necessary labour time so since to posit surplus labour, but comparatively the general devaluation of the necessary labour of society to a minimal, which thus correlates to the creative, scientific etc. development of the individuals in the time set free, and with the means to be creative, for all of them. Marx's theory of a post-capitalist communist society requires the free distribution of goods produced feasible by the abundance afforded by automation. The perfectly developed communist economic system is hypothesized to evolve from a preceding socialist systems. Marx held the view that socialism, a system based on social control of the systems of production would facilitate progress toward the development of comprehensively developed socialism by further accelerating effective technology. Under socialism, with its developing levels of automation, an increasing proportion of goods would be disseminated freely.

Karl Marx did not consider the eradication of most physical labor through technological improvements alone in a capitalist society, because he considered capitalism contained within it certain weaknesses which countered increasing automation and hindered it from establishing beyond a narrow objective, so that guide industrial labor could not be ignored until the crushing of Capitalism. Some critics on Marx have claimed that at the time he created the Grundrisse, he thought that the destruction of capitalism owing to advancing automation was inevitable despite these counter-inclinations, but that by the time of his significant work Capital: Critique of Political Economy he had withdrawn this view, and came to consider that capitalism would constantly renew itself unless overthrown. Normally, economists would acknowledge this is a positive thing. When the supply and demand curves for anything shift right, you have enhanced production but assuming proportional increments in supply and demand no inflation in prices. But my fear is at what human cost. Humans are not machines or widgets. And matter of fact, intellectual conversation and stimulation I consider is the most critical thing individuals can serve other humans, something physical components, let alone intelligent conversation. And so my second prediction.

Should post-scarcity ever occur, it will fragment humans into two camps.

1. Those willing to expend the effort necessary to participate in sex/attention
2. Those not willing to expend the effort and instead focus on intelligence and personality

The first group will likely breed and populate the future as their entire focus is on sex and attraction. The second group, though maybe not as much, will still copulate, but focus on less physical and more mental qualities and traits. Naturally, over time, these two groups will evolve with one group becoming "hotter" and the other group "uglier," but it makes me wonder if over time and because of the "hyper arms-sex-attention race" post scarcity would instill in the "hot group," that they would evolve into separate different species (and is here where my speculation runs out as I am not a great biologist, geneticist, let alone philosopher, and is perhaps where others might take over). However, as I said before, this was a mental exercise. There are many variables that would make such a scenario unlikely, even impossible, and I would hope some of you would point those out (besides, it would only take one generation focusing on looks and not the engineering needed to keep the 3d replicators operational that would end the post-scarcity economy). But before economists cheer for a post-scarcity economy, they may want to think about what it would replace and what the consequences might be. (D.Masley.2017)

In my My African Black book I go on to state that "I recommend that all companies should issue 20% shares to their Workforce in their annual profit allocation. My assertion is that employees contribute as much as the owners to ensure that their business remains profitable and hence should be compensated profitably appropriately too. Working and establishing another's person's dream at the current pay rate is economic enslavement in trickery and now everybody in the world is out to gain themselves on as much worthless paper-Money!!! Which has to be paid into a bank account, this money is then used by the Bankers to make more money while it sits in their bank accounts. This world is a Bankers paradise and they are the only ones profiting from everybody that is living. Inflation is another made up fallacy and currencies can be regulated by the confidence in the currency as an instrument of transaction as set by the national forces and should never be manipulated by foreign pressures. The London Currency Exchange centre and all European markets trading in African goods need to be put out of business, one question I would ask them is what is in England in terms of mineral wealth that makes their currency so strong? I live there and I know that all they have is Coal and Scottish Oil. Africa needs to set up their own African Reserve Bank without any Rothschild or private shares issued out. Shares must be issued to African states and its people. It should be run and controlled by the African Union, I do believe once Africa gets our currencies away from the hands of the Rothschild family we have a better chance of survival in this Global economy.(V.H Mnisi 2018)

European; American and Chinese economies are now massively reliant on their mineral rights that they have in Africa through their Multinational Corporations which are mainly controlled by graduates from one or more of these so called Secret Societies who assign their graduates into Political, Business and Religious positions of leadership. Our only economical hope from this abject poverty Africa finds itself in is African unification, Unity is strength which will emancipate Africans to command respect from the World. We need to consolidate Politically; Economically; Socially and Culturally like it's never been resolved or undertaken before. We Africans share one common theme and hold similar cultural values of Ubuntu and that should be the basis for our Unity. Africa demands a new kind of leadership and all of you here are the imminent leaders of tomorrow. Never look down at your dreams because it's your intuition and your personal God alerting you of what is conceivable. It's time now to create your dreams within your preferred academic field as this capitalistic world is constantly looking for slaves to exploit and my advice is never be intimidated not to change your mind and pick a different path. Change is desirable.

Our world has about 1260 quintillion liters of water. This means that 40 billion people using 200 liters a day each would help, over the course of a year, less than 0.00025% of the world's water...

"Be daring, be different, be impractical, be anything that will assert integrity of purpose and imaginative vision against the playitsafers, the creatures of the commonplace, the slaves of the ordinary"...By Cecil Beaton

Spiritual Abundant lifestyle

"Your purpose in life, you should have several which can be changed from time to time. One purpose everybody should have is making the world a better place. May your lives be at peace and may it overflow with peace, love and pure awesomeness today and everyday of your life. May the Sun bring you new energy by day and may the Moon restore you by night. May the breeze blow new strength into your being. May you walk gently through the world and know it's beauty all the days of your life." "God created humankind and gave them their rights to live their lives. With that right God gave humankind the power of discretion, which is the power to choose their own course of Action. Without discretion life is meaningless." "A Good life is when you smile often, dream big, laugh a lot and realise how blessed you are for what you have. Let your dreams be bigger than your fears and your actions speak louder than your words. Enjoy your life, for life is for us to live the best at what we are great at, so self-discover what you are born to do and make mint."

The Abundant Spiritual System "DRIVE CONFIDENTLY TOWARDS YOUR DREAMS, LIVE THE LIFE ONLY YOU CAN IMAGINE" By thaurus I own my time and command the space of my beingness, a space where I am allowed to grow into my true, unique nature. Success is a spiritual process, not a worldly one; that is to say it is an internal process, not external. It is a process of peeling off the layers of conditioning, becoming your essential truth, and living the inner-life. Success is, therefore, a process of honesty, and oftentimes, also one of courage...."There is no passion to be found playing small in settling for a life that is less than the one you are capable of living"....By Nelson Mandela this quote has made me think about my own situation and circumstances and I am thankful for my current situation as I have benefited from living the life in England, I enjoy it as I have been writing books for the last 10 years and I can only be grateful to God and my Ancestors for the inspirations and the motivation to accomplish every book venture..."This spiritual trinity manifests itself in the form of the Divine Light. Thus the essential element of both God and the human being is Light. Before birth and after death the human being exists as a light body which can travel from one planet to another at the speed of light"...By Kara Heritage Institute

"Be daring, be different, be impractical, be anything that will assert integrity of purpose and imaginative vision against the playitsafers, the creatures of the commonplace, the slaves of the ordinary"...By Cecil Beaton

The Wise book of Proverbs states and the only book I find worth reading in the King James Bible "Wine makes you mean, beer makes you quarrelsome, a staggering drunk is not much fun. Quick-tempered leaders are like mad dogs cross them and they bite your head off. It's a mark of good character to avert quarrels, but fools love to pick fights. A farmer too lazy to plant in the spring has nothing to harvest in the fall. Knowing what is right is like deep water in the heart; a wise person draws from the well within. Lots of people claim to be loyal and loving, but where on earth can you find one? God-loyal people, living honest lives, make it much easier for their children. Leaders who know their business and care keep a sharp eye out for the shoddy and cheap, For who among us can be trusted to always be diligent and honest? Switching price tags and padding the expense account are two things God hates.

Young people eventually reveal their actions if their motives are on the up and up. Ears that hear and eyes that see we get our basic equipment from God ! Don't be too fond of sleep; you'll end up in the poorhouse. Wake up and get up; then there'll be food on the table. The shopper says, "That's junk I'll take it off your hands," then goes off boasting of the bargain. Drinking from the chalice of knowledge is better than adorning oneself with gold and rare gems. Holding tight to a collateral on any loan to a stranger; beware of accepting what a transient has pawned. Stolen bread tastes sweet, but soon your mouth is full of gravel. Form your purpose by asking for counsel, then carry it out using all the help you can get. Gossips can't keep secrets, so never confide in blabbermouths.

Anyone who curses their father and mother extinguishes light and exists benighted. A bonanza at the beginning is no guarantee of blessing at the end. Don't ever say, "I'll get you for that!" Wait for God; he'll settle the score. It's easy to get distracted and unmotivated by negative opinion, however if you really intend working towards achieving something worthwhile, you have to stay true to your beliefs and aspirations no matter how insignificant they may seem to others. Long term strategies require a lot of patience and self-confidence, the best thing about them is you can always be proud of having made that effort to work towards achieving set objectives, it's always better to start and make mistakes along the way than to contemplate starting out of fear of being labelled a failure or associated with failure. "If you take responsibility and blame yourself, you have the power to change things. But if you put responsibility on someone else, then you are giving them the power to decide your fate." The best feeling in the world is finally knowing you took a step in the right direction. A step towards the future, Africa needs to start making a future for Africans like by writing this book now I feel great and inspired I am taking a step towards my future where everything is possible i.e I become a bestseller hopefully......As you start and end your day, be thankful for every little thing in your life. You will come to realize how blessed you truly are, It's time for Africans to awaken and embrace their own spirituality and Unite to become a formidable force in World Systematic Affairs.

"Good day to you, I hope you are enjoying the read, may your life! be at peace with itself, and may it overflow with peace, love and pure awesomeness today and everyday of your life! May God bring you new energy by day, and may he softly restore you by night too, May God wash away all your worries, and may your Ancestors blow new strength into your being. May you walk gently through the world and know it's beauty all the days of your life!" "God created humankind and gave them their rights to live their lives, with that right man was given the freedom to choose from many alternatives that surround their lives. God gave mankind the power of discretion, which is the power to choose their own course of action. Without discretion, life is meaningless. Hence Education is the foundation of fulfilling your Systematic Destiny. Choose your vocations wisely. You should always dream big and keep trying for that dream, never give up on your ambitions, I have accomplished most of my ambitions and I keep making bigger goals I hope to achieve. It's time, time to stop living your life because of what other people expect. It is time to walk your own path and follow your own dreams. Let go of your fears and always allow your heart to lead you, dont be told that you can't do this or you can't do that, be led by your heart but let your brains do the talking. Always know what you want to say, say no when you need to and always say yes when you need to also. Always have the confidence to say what you mean." "It's finally time to drop those negative thoughts about yourself; they are only getting in your way. Never mind whatever it is that you think you can't do, concentrate instead on what you can do. Always speak the truth even if our mind tells you otherwise and your voice shakes."

"Don't spend your whole life! looking for that one person to make you happy and complete because that one person is YOU!." The ability to speak several languages is an asset, but the ability to keeping your mouth shut in any language is priceless, sometimes peace and quiet prevails don't you just hate it when someone in the group keeps talking all the time and you feel like telling them to shut up!

Love more. Dream Big, Laugh Lots and have Faith that your dreams will prevail and keep working on them daily. "My advice is never to do tomorrow what you can do today. Procrastination is the thief of time", this is so true and I live by it. "I personally experienced it when I told myself that I will do something tomorrow it never gets done, you normally forget about it as every day brings Different Systematic Vibes so if you feel the Systematic Vibrations off doing something just do it and get it over and done with it." "Everybody has many flaws, nobody is perfect and every successful man has failed many times before making it. Always tell yourself that I have too many blessings to be ungrateful. Always be Happy and Bright. Always Be You!"

The distance between your dreams and reality is called action. You should always act on your intuition; you never know where it may lead you to. You need to forget what's gone and appreciate what still remains and always look forward to what's coming next. Don't start your day with the broken pieces of yesterday. Every day is a fresh start. Each day is a new beginning. Every morning we wake up is the first day of our new Life!. "Be of good cheer, it's still a fabulous year!. Don't give up. Keep going. You will soon find your happiness just keep going and keep trying because happiness is the brightest level of everybody's success story." "Be always optimistic as it is the one quality most associated with success and happiness than any other." As optimism keeps the soul going and keeps it longing for more. "Success is no accident. It is hard work, perseverance, learning, studying, sacrifice and most of all loving what you are doing or learning to do". Dig deep down in your soul and you will find what you were born to do just keep digging that path you will find your light as the path of the righteous is like the light of Dawn, which shines Brighter and Brighter in your Soul. We are each gifted in a unique and important way and it is our privilege and our adventure to discover our own Special Light System. Light up your World System by Soul Searching,

"As days are different, some great and some bad. Some days you may wonder how you survived, and held on this long, but always remind yourself that with struggle comes strength. There is no joy without knowing struggle." Always keep a smile on your face it may catch on. "Take nothing for granted everyday is a blessing, embrace the struggles. Let it make you stronger for success. Your blessings are on the way! And Nothing ever goes away until it teaches us what we need to know so embrace your struggles too and learn from them. You are not born a winner and you're not born a loser. You are born a chooser. Decide once and for all to have an extraordinary life! Because whatever you believe with conviction becomes reality. Always believe in your dreams."

Sometimes all you need is a hundred million dollars don't we all wish for that big win? I always say to myself that if you are not in you can't win it. Keep getting your lottery tickets and keep betting on your numbers because once I placed a lucky dip and my numbers came out I mean really my date of birth numbers 29/03/19/30/40 imagine that all my five came out when I got the lucky dip that's my luck hay? Every morning start a new page in your life-story and always create a great day, in fact make everyday a great day. Always take out time to pray and contemplate your day. It helps with your creativity. Always take time to breathe and realise how blessed you are to be alive. "Never hinder your inner First Creative Voice driving, be creative and never listen to the Second Voice telling you that the dream is impossible, always listen to the First Voice off your Intuition".

"Creative people are easily bored, take risks, colour outside the lines. Creative people think with their hearts and make lots of mistakes. Creative people hate the rules and always want to work alone so they can change their mind if they need to. Creative people have a reputation for eccentricity and always dream big. " Alway have good thoughts as they will shine out of your face like sunbeams and you will always look lovely, be friendly to everybody and smile to everyone you meet. Once you connect with yourself it is impossible to be lonely or desperate. You get to live your life according to your terms which I believe is good for you. It's never too late to start doing the right thing. Start now, forgive, love again, start your life! anew again. Whatever it is you need to do, just do it. There is no need holding on to past hurts let it go. Revive your light, manifest your dreams, realise your self worth, stop hanging on to yesterday's problems and discover your today's opportunities instead.

This Capitalistic Systematic World we live in now is not created to be fair. It's built on the ethos of a dog eat dog world. If you expect the world to be fair with you because you are fair, you're fooling yourself. That's like expecting the lions not to eat you because you don't eat them."The most important thing to realise is yourself worth. When you know your worth you set the standards for you". Never allow problems to push you into negative thoughts about yourself. As problems will only weigh down your dreams, always be led by your dreams. Believe that you can make it and you will make it. Always aim to be Happy! You must become a happiness seeker. You have to always think about happiness, look out for happiness and always believe with all your heart that you deserve happiness. "Happiness is knowing and believing that you are fabulous. know that you are always Fabulous everyday! and let happiness have her fabulous way in your life! Today and everyday of your life!"

Always have a great attitude towards your daily chores because it builds up a great mood and feeling. As a great mood becomes a great day. A great day becomes a great week, a great week becomes a great month which makes it a great life! Always do the right thing, "Integrity is doing the right thing when nobody's watching". Be patient with your goals and dreams as some creations take time. Give the seeds of your dreams time to take root and find their way into the world. It's OK to take out time to nourish your soul and let the universe work its magic just let God do his work in you. Keep yourself updated with the latest trends and educate yourself in the field that you are interested in, use the internet and create your Systematic Digital Footprint. We are in the age of Information Technology, Ignorance is a Choice.

Dear whoever is reading this, I hope you have a reason to smile today. "Have a good day! May your hearts overflow with peace, love and pure awesomeness today and enjoy the read and get Inspired! I hope you have some adventures and discoveries this week. I hope you discover something new. I hope you get to see and meet some beautiful people today. And I hope you feel at peace all the way through". Always pray to your Ancestor to guide your daily footsteps building self confidence which is nothing more than believing in yourself, it is also about doing the things you once didn't believe you could do. God lives in us, in everybody you can find God's Natural Systems living in them, our souls houses the living God, we as humans must be glad that our reflection in the mirror is like looking at the image of God as he made each one of us in his own image.

"Friends are the family we choose for ourselves, they are like the sunshine that brightens up our day and I bet you that if you pray to God to protect you from your enemies, that you will start losing people you thought were your friends." Choose your friends wisely because you could be let down, I recall a time in Harare Zimbabwe while attending Allan Wilson Boys School I told a close friend who has passed away now Dumisane Gutu R.I.P my brother about an incident that happened to me while I was drunk and he told everybody he knew. Yesterday I was clever, so I wanted to change the world, today I am wiser, so I am changing myself. A perfect person doesn't smoke, doesn't drink, doesn't cry, doesn't fail and doesn't exit. Judging people does not make you any better. Life's too short to argue and fight. Count your blessings, value your friends and move on with your head held high and smile for everyone you meet. Fighting has never solved anything, especially physical engagement and verbal engagement can be very harmful to the soul. Mind your words because they can hurt as bad as a thrown spear straight to the heart and soul of any Person's Personal System.

"You cannot hang out with negative people and expect to live a positive life." "Avoid negative people, for they are the greatest destroyers of self-confidence and self-esteem, surround yourself with people who bring out the best in you" Choose the people you spend your time with very carefully. Family isn't always blood, it's the people in your life who want you in theirs; the ones who accept you for who you are, the ones who would do anything to see you smile and who love you no matter what. You see a person's true colours when you are no longer beneficial to their life. They suddenly change the behaviour towards you. I ditch those kinds of people and avoid them like the plague. "I don't care about losing people who don't wanna be in my life anymore. I've lost people who meant the world to me and I am still doing fine". "I don't know the key to success, but the key to failure is to try to please everyone."

Become friends with people who aren't your age, I have always had older close friends than me ever since being a teenager I have hung around with much older people. Hang out with people whose first language isn't the same as yours. That's how you learn to communicate better and learn other people's cultures too. Get to know someone who doesn't come from your social class, learn to mix with everybody and learn to fit in everywhere. This is how you see the world. This is how you grow. Always speak when you are angry, never keep anger inside you will never regret it. Just speak tactfully and calmly explaining your anger to the person that has made you angry. Tact is the ability to tell someone to go to hell in such a way that they look forward to the trip.

"Sometimes our lives have to be completely shaken up, changed, and rearranged to relocate us to the place we are meant to be". God will allow you to go through painful periods so you can enjoy winning the battles he put in our way to conquer. Those who sow in tears shall reap in joy, don't worry, things will work out soon. Just keep your strength in good thoughts. People who have good thoughts cannot ever be ugly. You can have a wonky nose and a crooked mouth and a double chin and stick-out teeth, but if you have good thoughts they will shine out of your face like sunbeams and you will always look lovely. You should always surround yourself with only people who are going to lift you higher. Never hang around people that put you down and make you feel inadequate. "People were created to be loved; things were created to be used. The reason why this world is in chaos is because things are being loved and people are being used." Learn to see people for their self worth, not what they have and what you can get from them.

"I fall, I rise, I make mistakes, I live, I learn, I am not perfect but I am thankful"."When the blood in your veins returns to the sea, and the earth in your bones returns to the ground, perhaps then you will remember that this land does not belong to you, it is you who belongs to this land." Be the reason someone smiles today. Make an old friend smile today, send them a text, Facebook chat with them or just call them now. It's been said that everlasting friends go long periods of time without speaking and never question their friendship. These friends pick up phones like they just spoke yesterday, regardless of how long it has been or how far away they live and they don't hold grudges. They understand that life is busy and you will always love them. I just love my friends all over the world.

"The world's going to judge you no matter what you do, so live life! the way you want and enjoy every moment. I don't live my life! to please anyone, I don't care what anyone thinks. If you don't like me, don't talk to me, problem solved". Right!?Right! "I think it's very healthy to spend time alone. You need to know how to be alone and not be defined by another person". You have to discover yourself first before you can give yourself totally to another person. You have to be happy with yourself first before you can make anybody happy to be with you. "Happiness starts with you, not with your relationship, not with your job, not with your money, but with you.

"Be thankful for what you have; you will end up having more. If you concentrate on what you don't have, you will never ever have enough". Two things define you: Your patience when you have nothing, and your attitude when you have everything. "Happiness is not something that you get in life. Happiness is rather something that you bring to life. Bring your happiness in every situation you get involved in. "Sometimes you have to move on without certain people, If they are meant to be in your life, they will catch up" believe in your journey without them. "It's during the worst times of your life that you will get to see the true colours of the people who say they care for you". "Everything happens for a reason, maybe you don't see the reason right now, but when it is finally revealed it will blow you away. "The truth does not change because it is, or is not believed by the majority of the people. "The truth will always remain the truth and it will set you free" Always aim to tell the truth every time it will save you from explaining yourself when the truth is revealed as the truth will always reveal itself someday. "The most dangerous liars are those who think they are telling the truth". Don't you just hate being lied to?

The worst person to be around is someone who complains about everything and appreciates nothing. We are all going to die someday, all of us, that alone should make us love each other but it doesn't. We are rather terrorized and flattened by trivialities of the world, we are all absorbed up by nothing. "When your past calls don't answer. It has nothing new to say. Stop looking at your   past mistakes always look forward to your next venture. You have to speak to be heard, but sometimes you have to be silent to be appreciated. The most hurtful thing you can say to someone is to say nothing.

"If you want to live a happy life, tie it to a goal, not to people and things". Sometimes I forget to thank the people who make my life happy in many ways. Sometimes I forget to tell them how much I really do appreciate them for being an important part of my life. So thank you for reading this book. "Everybody has a good story to tell about their life" write your story. Keep a diary of your daily occurrence for eyes you will learn to cover your purpose in life! Pray for God to save you from your mental state you may find yourself in. "But before an individual can be saved, he must first learn that he cannot save himself". Always learn from people as Life is short, there is no time to leave important words unsaid and done. Sometimes the more chances you give the more respect you lose. Never let a person get comfortable with disrespecting you. "Some people come in your life as blessings, others come in your life as lessons. Returning hate for hate multiplies hate, adding deeper darkness to a night already devoid of stars. "People think being alone makes you lonely, but I don't think that's true, being surrounded by the wrong people is the loneliest thing in the world". "Life is better when you're laughing but there are times when you have to be sad and blue" It has been said that "Good things come to those who believe, better things come to those who are patient and the best things come to those who don't give up". Stop speaking about your ambitions just do them and let them do the talking for you. "May your life! preach more loudly than your lips".

Take care of your thoughts when you are alone, and take care of your words when you are with people". As the saying goes, keep your thoughts pure for the bad thoughts are lurking around to jump on the bad ones. As I have learnt that you should always listen to the first thought and never the second. I have been practising it ever since and I now feel much closer to my Spirit as he guides me daily through my chores and we speak like old friends isn't that amazing that I have a spirit with me all this time?. My Spirit is informing me now that telepathic communication is possible through him with people who have him as a companion. WOW!!! Isn't that just so great to know, I am going to try it.

"Our culture has accepted two huge lies, first is that if you disagree with someone's lifestyle, you must fear or hate them. The second is that to love someone means you must agree with everything they believe in or do. Both are nonsense. You don't have to compromise convictions to be compassionate". Don't be driven by approval fixes, do the best you can, be the best that you can be and do not feel you should be able to do more than just because someone else does more. Just be yourself, and don't pressure yourself to perform exactly the way others do. There are people who have plotted against you who still don't know how you survived. Real situations expose fake people, rock bottom will always reveal what's real. Your hardest times will expose your truest friendships, Rock bottom will always reveal who's real. Know your circle. Sometimes you just need to disconnect and enjoy your own company. Let wisdom be your sister and knowledge your friend.

Wanted: Encourages (We have a surplus of critics already, thanks.   "All views are entitled to be aired just Messenger me on Vincent Happy Mnisi. Because It is through vigorous and constructive debate that together we will chart the path ahead. Whoever controls the media, controls the culture". The internet has broken that myth and is interconnecting the world producing a global culture. "When your earnings are exhausted on food and shelter, your labours are no longer viewed as an opportunity for economic advancement, but rather as an act of self-preservation. In the real world, that's called slavery. "If you think adventure is dangerous, try routine, it is lethal". "Finish every day, and be done with it. You have done what you could, some blunders and absurdities no doubt crept in; forget them as fast as you can, tomorrow is a new day. You shall begin it well and with high spirit too. Just get on with your day and do what needs to be done. Just get on with it!

10 ways to move on 1) Allow yourself to be happy always. 2) Be confident and trust yourself always. 3) Welcome change and go with it always. 4) Be courageous and take risks all the time. 5) Ditch the guilt, it will weigh you down. 6) Know that you deserve the best and always aim to be the best. 7) Make a decision on what you want to do and follow it through. 8) Smile in the face of adversity it will only last just a while. 9) Remember that you are good enough and you deserve everything you aim for. 10) Be yourself always. People come and go from our lives all the time, it is not our fault that people leave. The universe is just making room for new people with new lessons. Life! becomes easier when you learn to accept the apology you never got and If you are doing the best you can under your current circumstances then kick up your heels and dance enjoy the moment go to a concert go watch a movie and enjoy your life!.

True friends don't believe rumours about you because they know you. True friends defend you, and never spread lies about you. People who spread rumours will be ruined too. Sometimes the Bad things that happen in our lives put us directly on the path to the best things that will ever happen to us. "When the world says "Give up" Hope whispers "One more time". The secret to change is to focus all your energy, not on fighting the old, but on building the new". If you want to live your dreams, you have to give up all your excuses. Ego says "Once everything falls into place, I will find peace" Spirit says "Find peace and everything will fall into place". If you want to reach a goal, you must see yourself reaching that goal in your mind before you actually arrive at your goal. Goal setting is great, it's difficult so plan well and just go for it, Just Do it you will learn on the way how to do it properly. "Once you feel you are avoided by someone, never disturb them again. Just do your thing and get your hustle on. Hard work is easy, working out is hard. There are something's that money cannot buy, like manners, morals, intelligence and class. "I found the key to happiness is staying away from idiots". "Try being informed instead of just opinionated. And tell the negative committee that meets inside your head to sit down and shut up. Success means doing the best we can with what we have. Success is the doing, not the getting; in the trying, not the triumph. Success is personal standards reaching for the highest that is in us, becoming all that we can be. The strongest factor for success is self-esteem, believing you can do it, believing you deserve it, believing you will get it. Life is give and take, don't lose the battle in your mind. Always remember; the more life stresses you, the more life will have to bless you. Get ready to receive your blessings. Successful people build each other up, they motivate, inspire and push each other. Unsuccessful people just hate, blame and complain. Fake people don't surprise me anymore, loyal people do. "In the end, we only regret the chances we didn't take, relationships we were afraid to have, and the decisions we waited too long to make". "Choose to win each day, defy the odds, embrace all challenges that you face, and never let adversity steal your dreams". A change begins in your mind. If you are grateful for even one thing in your life right now, there is no need to regret the past because it brought you here, embrace your journey. You can't play it safe your whole life and expect to reach your highest potential. You've got to be willing to take some risk. Weak people revenge, strong people forgive, intelligent people ignore.

"When people don't know what's going on in your life, they speculate, when they think they know they fabricate and when they do know. They just hate. " "Never give up on what you really want to do, the person with big dreams is more powerful than one with facts. Having a friend who understands your tears is much more valuable than having a bunch of friends who only know your smile. Always tell yourself "I'm strong, I'm resilient, I'm trying my best, I value my life, I'm not perfect, I'm the perfect me, I never give up, I am empathetic, I am a warrior ready to conquer. I am not broken, I am together. I take things one day at a time, I'm independent, I'm human and I'm a survivor."

"The person you took for granted today, may turn out to be the person you need tomorrow, be careful how you treat people". Spiritually, it's important to forgive those who hurt you, but you don't need to hang out with them. The biggest communication problem is we do not listen to understand, instead we listen to reply. "You may not control all the events that happen to you, but you can decide not to be reduced by them. We are very good lawyers for our own mistakes, but very good Judges for the mistakes of others. Never trust anyone who always blames everyone else for everything wrong in their life. Not everything that is faced can be changed, but nothing can be changed until it is faced. "I was raised! I didn't just grow up, I was taught to speak when I enter a room. Say please and thank you, to have respect for my elders and to get up off my lazy butt, let them have my chair", Say "Yes sir" and "No sir", "lend a helping hand to those in need. Hold the door for the person behind me, say excuse me when it's needed, and to love people for who they are and not for what I can get from them, I was also taught to treat people the way I want to be treated". "It does not matter if a million people tell you what you can't do, or if 10 million tell you No!" If you get one "Yes" from God, that's all you need. Just keep praying for him to answer you through your Holy Spirit" who is always by your side and have faith.

I regret nothing in my life even if my past was full of disappointments, I still look back and smile, because it made me who I am today. Never regret your past as it was a lesson from God. Always be ready for the next lesson. When you do the right thing in the right way, you have nothing to lose because you have nothing to fear. You have never really lived until you have done something for someone who can never repay you. Always be a helping hand to the needy. Many people, especially ignorant people, want to punish you for speaking the truth, for being correct, or for being years ahead of your time. If you are right and you know it, speak your mind. Even if you are a minority of one, the truth is still the truth. The way you dress yourself and portray yourself to the world says plenty about who you are and how you want the world to accept you. Always dress to impress as you never know whom you shall meet. You should venture out in life everyday looking for opportunities to improve yourself as you never know what you can achieve until you have pushed yourself to your limit as success is no accident, it is hard work; perseverance; learning; studying; sacrifice and most of all loving what you are doing or learning to do".

Never look back and wonder why things went wrong, don't regret not doing more, it happened for a reason, your better days are ahead of you. Forget about all the reasons why something may not work, you only need to find one reason why it will. I will no longer allow the negative things in my life to spoil all of the good things I have, I choose to be happy. I would rather be anointed by God than to be popular. The first to apologize is the bravest, the first to forgive is strongest, and the first to forget is the happiest.

"Stop holding on to the wrong people. Let them go on their way; if not for you, then for them. Accept the person and the situation for exactly what it is instead of trying to manipulate it into what you think it needs to be." "When writing the story of your life, don't let anyone else hold the pen". "The best way to predict the future; it's to create one yourself". Call me crazy but I love to see other people happy and succeeding. Life is flying by, you don't have time to waste another minute being negatively offended or bitter. If someone did you wrong, get over it and move on with your life!. I'm making some changes in my life!. If you don't hear anything from me, you are one of them. I don't have to agree with you to like you or respect you. I actually don't need to control my anger. Everyone around me needs to control their habits of pissing me off. "I have learned the value in experience, though I haven't always seen things clear, I'm now thankful for things I never imagined I could be. If it wasn't for the liars, I wouldn't know the value of peace. If it wasn't for the good things failing, I wouldn't know what was needed to set the foundations for something great. I have learnt the power of acceptance through my disappointments. Every let-down has left me in a position to grow, and I'm wiser because of it all. I am proud of my heart, it's never been a quitter, it hasn't become bitter, it's had the courage to stay open, and that has only made me a better person indeed".

"There is no passion to be found playing small in settling for a life that is less than the one you are capable of living". "Do not judge me by my successes, judge me by how many times I fell down and got back up again." "There is no need to rush, if something is meant to be, it will happen at the right time, with the right person for the right reasons." Happiness does not depend on what you have or who you have in your life; it solely relies on what you think. Everything you're going through is preparing you for what you asked for. Wealth makes friends, but the poor are separated from their friends. Book of Proverbs. If you are under attack, it's because your blessing is close; thieves only come to loaded vaults, stay encouraged. Always pray to have eyes that see the best, a heart that forgives the worst, a mind that forgets the bad and a soul that never loses faith. You will never understand a person until you consider things from their point of view, until you climb into their skin and walk around in it. You have permission to walk away from anything that doesn't feel right. Trust your instincts and listen to your inner voice. It's trying to protect you. Stop holding onto people who keep letting go of you. Pay attention to the faithful people. The ones you don't have to impress, the ones who always have your back. The ones that love you with no strings attached. The best way to avoid disappointment is not to expect anything from anyone. Never cry for that person who doesn't know the value of your tears.

I fall, I rise. I make mistakes. I live. I learn. I've been hurt but I'm alive. I'm human. I'm not perfect but I'm thankful. I believe in second chances, I don't think everyone deserves them. Such a disappointment when you defend someone for so long thinking they are different and they turn out to be just like what everyone said. Some people you have to leave them to their ways. If they can't appreciate you then let them miss you. Absence makes the heart grow fonder; But if it doesn't grow fonder, at least yours will grow stronger. I don't let people pull me into their storm; I pull them into my peace. The only people I owe my loyalty to those who never made me question theirs. One of the biggest lessons I have learned from my journeys is you can't please everyone so don't try. Surround yourself with people who clearly love your light and add to it. "Some people are allergic to nuts. Some people are allergic to milk, Me? I am allergic to lies and negativity". Successful people build each other up, they motivate, inspire and push each other. Unsuccessful people just hate, blame and complain. Fake people don't surprise me anymore, loyal people do. When you're dead, you don't know you're dead it's the same way when you're stupid. People often say that motivation doesn't last. Well neither does bathing. That's why we recommend it daily. Always help someone, you might be the only one who does. Other people and things can stop you temporarily. You're the only one who can do it permanently.

Nourish your soul by spending time with people that celebrate who you are, and avoid those that simply you tolerate. You are worth more than that. If you feel ignored, you're probably doing everything right. Direction is so much more important than speed. Many are going nowhere very fast. There comes a time when you have to stop crossing oceans for people who wouldn't jump puddles for you. F.R.I.E.N.D.S stands for: F: Fight for you. R: Respect you. I: Include you. E: Encourage you. N: Need you. D: Deserve you. And S: Stand by you. Hear me when I tell you this: People who ignore you, until it suits them to talk to you, are not worth your friendship or your time!. The best kind of people are the ones that come into your life, and make you see the sun where you once saw clouds. The people that believe in you so much, you start to believe in you too. The people that love you simply for being you. The once in a lifetime kind of people.

Just be honest with me or stay away from me. It's not that difficult. People will question all the good things they hear about you but believe all the bad without a second thought typical of people. Don't waste words on people who deserve your silence. Sometimes the most powerful thing you can say is nothing at all. You teach people how to treat you by what you allow, what you stop, and what you reinforce. I love straight people, they make life ten times easier. If you set yourself free from what everyone else thinks and start being who you were created to be, you will rise to a new level. When we are kind to ourselves and one another, we create heaven on earth. When you find yourself in a position to help someone, be happy and feel blessed because God is answering that person's prayer, through you. Remember: Our purpose on earth is not to get lost in the dark but to be a light to others, so that they may find their way through us. God bless you!. "What is one thing you can do right now to make someone's day better? Just Do it.

Everyone has experienced something that has changed them in a way that they could never go back to the person they once were. Everyone has experienced sorrow and happiness. Always stay true to yourself and never let what somebody else distract you from your goals. In the end, people will judge you anyway. Don't live your life impressing others. Live your life impressing yourself. Be careful who you trust. If someone will discuss others with you, they will certainly discuss you with others. Your circles of friends must match your own aspirations and dreams, or you will find little support when you need it most. "The saddest thing about betrayal is that it never comes from your enemies. The person you trust may turn out to be your worst enemy, be careful of who you tell your secrets. I have learnt my lesson.

You can't use people and expect God to keep blessing you. Some of the things we hold on to the most are the things we need to let go of the most. Remember that criticism, negativity, spitefulness are only reflections of the person giving them. You don't have to accept them. If you want to fly, you have to give up the things that weigh you down." Never be afraid to raise your voice for honesty and truth and compassion. Speak loudly against injustice, lying and greed. If people all over the world did this, it would change the world. Ego and greed work very well with each other, they are both never satisfied with what they have. If you want to make peace with an enemy, one must work with that enemy and that enemy becomes your partner. When someone tells you, "You've changed" It might simply be because you've stopped living your life their way. You can still be a good friend and say "No". Sometimes we need to balance our desire to care for others with our own personal needs. Don't give yourself away! It is your job to like you.

"My belief in Social Justice Systems means that I believe in equality, in the dignity and value of all human lives. It means that sometimes not everything is about me. It means that sometimes, you need to have a seat and listen". There's a difference between knowing somebody and hearing about somebody. Just because you heard, doesn't mean you know them. Don't you just hate it when some people keep talking about other people. People are confused about forgiveness; it's not about excusing someone's actions. It's about not allowing their actions to hurt you anymore. Stop comparing yourself to others, you have your own race to run. Finish well. People who judge you by your past, don't belong in your present. I like rumours, I find out so much about me that I didn't even know. When you begin to attract people who support you, your dreams are beginning to unfold. Whenever I feel weak, I'll remember those who make me strong and whenever I start to doubt myself, I'll remember those who believe in me. Nobody is too busy; it's just a matter of priorities." We cannot teach people anything; we can only help them discover it within themselves. Let us not forget that it is friendship, always friendship, that is the great source and wellspring of fun in our lives. Knowing a person is like music, what attracts us to them is their melody, and as we get to know who they are, we learn their lyrics.

Don't Chase people, Be yourself, do your own thing, and work hard. The right people. The ones who really belong in your life will come to you and stay. Better be slapped with the truth, than kissed with a lie always tell the truth even if it hurts. I hate it when you have to be nice to someone you really want to throw a brick at them. Don't let other people's behaviour destroy your inner peace. Never get upset with people or situations, both are powerless without your reaction.

My Happiness does not depend upon anyone else's. I promised myself to make all my friends feel that there is something worthwhile in them. You are in charge of how you react to the people and events in your life. You can either give negativity power over your life or you can choose happiness instead. Don't allow anyone to take you for granted you are too valuable to not be appreciated. Some people don't know how to appreciate a friend because they don't know how to be one. All friends are not true, but true friends are very few. Do what you can to help people but have the wisdom to accept your limits. Be mindful of where you pledge your allegiance, sometimes it's hard to tell friend from foe. Grades don't measure intelligence and age doesn't define maturity. Remember that guys that gave up? Neither does anybody else. You cannot save everyone. Some people are going to destroy themselves no matter how much you try to help them. Life is too short to wake up in the morning with regrets. So love the people who treat you right, forgive the ones who don't and I believe everything happens for a reason.

Minding your own business goes far beyond simply avoiding the temptation to try and solve other people's problems. It also includes eavesdropping; gossiping; talking behind other people's backs and analysing or trying to figure out other people. One of the Major Systemic reasons most of us focus on the shortcomings or problems of others is to avoid looking at ourselves. Don't be judgemental. When you hold resentment towards another, you are bound to that person or condition by an emotional link that is stronger than steel. Forgiveness is the only way to dissolve that link and get free. Always forgive but never forget. Always help someone when you can help out. You might be the only one who does. When other people treat you poorly, walk away, smile and keep being you. Don't ever let someone else's bitterness change the person you are. Some people don't like you because your strength reminds them of their weakness. Don't let their hate slow you down. The moment you feel like you have to prove your worth to someone is the moment to absolutely and utterly walk away. Your job isn't to Judge. Your job isn't to figure out if someone deserves something or decide who is right or wrong. Your Job is to lift the fallen, restore the broken and heal the hurting.

We are all equal whether one is rich or poor, educated or illiterate; religious or non believing, man or woman; black, white or brown we all the same. Physically, Emotionally and Mentally we are all equal. We all share basic needs for Food; Shelter; Safety and Love. We all Aspire to Happiness and we all Shun Suffering. Each of us has Hopes, Worries, Fears and Dreams. Each of us wants the best for our family and loved ones. We all experience pain when we suffer loss and joy when we achieve what we seek. On this Fundamental Systematic level, Religion, Ethnicity, Culture and Languages makes no difference.

Not every person is going to understand you and that's okay. They have a right to their opinion and you have every right to ignore it. Be you no matter what. The idea is not to see through one another, but to see one another through. Be open to others; give people a chance. Be open to yourself; give yourself a chance. The key is to keep company only with people who uplift you, whose presence calls forth your best. The whole world can love you, but that love will not make you happy. What will make you happy is the love coming out of you. The most beautiful people we have known are those who have known defeat, known suffering, known struggle, known loss, and have found their way out of the depths. These people have an appreciation, a sensitivity, and an understanding of life that fills them with compassion, gentleness and a deep loving concern. Beautiful people do not just happen. Be kind, gentle and loving towards everyone you meet. When I offer loving kindness to others something happens to my own heart. I feel it right there inside of me. Each time I extend love. I feel my Spiritual System Growing closer to the truth. Being Considered crazy by those who are still victims of cultural conditioning is a compliment.

Forgiveness doesn't mean trusting someone again. Forgiveness doesn't mean put yourself in harm's way again. Forgiveness doesn't mean justice is served. Forgiveness means you get your freedom back. Do something wonderful, people may imitate it. Stop getting attached to people so fast, because attachments lead to expectations and expectations lead to disappointments. If you are who you are it is really hard to steal and before you diagnose yourself with depression or low self esteem, first make sure that you are not in fact, surrounded by negative people. We would do ourselves a tremendous favour by letting go of the people who poison our Spiritual System. Sometimes you have to accept the truth and stop wasting precious time on the wrong people. Fools take a knife and stab people in the back. The wise take a knife, cut the cord and free themselves from the fools. Some people are so addicted to their misery that they will destroy anything that gets in the way of their fix. No man or woman is an island. Ask for help, for what you need. Everyone has their own path. Walk yours with integrity and wish all others peace on their journeys. When your paths merge, rejoice for their presence in your life. When your paths are separated, return to the wholeness of yourself, give thanks for their footprints left on your soul, and embrace the time to journey on your own. Sometimes a person needs us to abandon them, but we hang on anyway, which can be devastating for both parties don't you just hate Toxic Relationships Systems?

Helping others can sometimes even be a convenient distraction from addressing our own unresolved issues. When someone you know is so toxic and destructive, that they are poisoning your life, You have to create some distance. They need you to walk away as much as you need it too. Try to avoid them. If people say something bad about you, judge you as if they know you. Don't get affected. Remember that dogs bark if they don't know the person. You learn from other people you spend most of your time choosing wisely. You become like the people you spend the most time with choose wisely!. "Never lose faith in humanity. Humanity is like an ocean; If a few drops of the ocean are dirty, the ocean does not become dirty. Live your life in every way to earn and keep the respect of the people you respect". What did you learn yesterday? And more importantly, what did you teach to someone else yesterday? What you give away will multiply in your life. I have learned that it is not what I have in my life but who I have in my life that counts.

Practice forgiveness always, to let others know that you no longer wish to be in a state of hostility with them and to free yourself from the Self-Defeating Energy Systems of resentment. Send love in some form to those you feel have wronged you and notice how much better you feel. Finding your passion isn't just about careers and money. It's about finding your authentic self. The one you've buried beneath other people's needs. Not everyone will share your vision. That still does not mean that there is something wrong with your sight. As long as you can sweeten another's pain, life is not in vain. Just being there for someone can sometimes bring hope when all seems hopeless. Hold yourself responsible for a higher standard than anybody else expects of you. Never excuse yourself. Never pity yourself. Be a hard master to yourself and lenient to everybody else. I have learned that it's not what I have in my life but who I have in my life that counts. If someone has offended you, insulted you, or disappointed you, let it go! If you are remembering all the ways you have been hurt or forgotten, let it go! Ask yourself? what good does it do for me to hold on to this. There is a nobility in compassion, a beauty in empathy, a grace in forgiveness. Blessed are those who can give without remembering and take without forgetting. Some of the most amazing people in the world were not perfect; they were scarred by suffering, hardship, losses and imperfections. But when they recovered they were stronger, wiser and more loving and compassionate. Your life is going to get better in the proper time, and you will be stronger and more at peace than ever before.

Move on to the good stuff. If you have a bite of something nasty, you leave it and nibble on the other stuff that tastes good, right? So when someone has a negative thing to say brush it off move on, don't chew on it spit it out! Say "Thank you", enjoy and appreciate the nice things that are said to you. Compliments taste much better don't they?. You can't please everybody so don't even try. No time is better spent than in the service of others. Don't take me for granted because unlike others I am not afraid to walk away. We judge people today by their actions. We don't know that actions on the outside can be different to actions on the inside. Because of this we don't know our friends and our enemies. Know your worthiness, know when you have had enough of something. And keep moving from people who ruin your happiness. You don't ever have to feel guilty about removing toxic people from your life. It doesn't matter whether someone is a relative, romantic interest, employer, childhood friend or a new acquaintance. You don't have to make room for people who cause you pain or make you feel small. It's one thing if a person owns up to their behaviour and makes an effort to change. But if a person disregards your feelings, ignores your boundaries, and continues to treat you in a harmful way, they need to go. Attract what you expect, reflect what you desire, become what you expect, mirror what you admire. Some people are going to reject you, simply because you shine too bright for them. And that's okay. Keep shining. I am only responsible for what I say not for what you understand. The older I get, the less I care about what people think of me. Therefore the older I get, the more I enjoy life.

I am not a perfect person. I make a lot of mistakes. But I really appreciate those people who stay with me after knowing how I really am. Good people give you happiness, Bad people give you experience. Worst people give you a lesson and Best people give you memories. Try not to take things personally, what people say about you is a reflection of them, not you. Don't let anyone else's fears, limitations or sense of lack determine how you live your life. You can't let people scare you. You can't go your whole life trying to please everyone else. You can't go through life worried about what everyone else is going to think. Whether it's your hair, clothes, whatever you have to say how you feel, what you believe and what you have. You can't let the judgement of others stop you from being you. Because if you do, you're no longer you, you're someone everyone else wants you to be. Seeking the approval of others will never bring you happiness. You don't need anybody's permission, You have to trust in your own value if you want others to recognise your value. When someone is vicious towards you they are giving you a glimpse of the pain they are carrying in themselves. A hot tempered man stirs up dissension, but a patient man calms a quarrel. You can't make someone become something they aren't ready to be. If they won't grow with you, be willing to grow without them. As soon as you stop comparing yourself with others, you are free to enjoy being you. Open minded people do not feel the need to impose their Belief Systems. Closed minded people believe it's their way or it's the wrong way. Which are you?.

The sign of a beautiful person is that they always see beauty in others. Learn to be alone and to like it. There is nothing more freeing and empowering than learning to like your own company. Sometimes walking away has nothing to do with weakness, and everything to do with strength. We walk away not because we want others to realise our value and worth. But because we finally realise our own worthiness. Everything you say to someone else is for your clarity not theirs. You are presenting yourself, to yourself, for yourself at every moment. Never confuse education with intelligence. It's not the colour of our skin that makes us different, It's the colour of our thoughts. Never underestimate the power of Stupid people in large groups, look at Donald Trump is now the President of America and what is happenned with the recent racist killings feuled by his hate speeches and rethoric fuled by the ANC leadership thesed 2019 Xenophobia Crimes in South Africa. Be kind, for everyone you meet is fighting a battle you know nothing about. Some people are like clouds, when they go it's a beautiful day. A negative thinker sees difficulty in every opportunity, a positive thinker sees an opportunity in every difficulty. Rules are for people who don't know what to do. Think for yourself, question everything? Live in such a way that if someone spoke badly of you, no one would believe it. "In life, sometimes getting hurt is a necessary path, Do not deny yourself of this experience, but never dwell in it. You have to go through it and not around it for you to get over it. "I gave my all still they said it wasn't enough. I tried to do better still they magnified my flaws. I put others before me and still they said I was selfish. I showed them my heart, still they only saw my past. I shared my story. Still they ridiculed my mistakes. I told them my dreams, still they laughed at my visions. I gave my life to God still they pointed out my sins. But through it all I've realised. I'm here to please God, not them". "Our lives are storybooks that we write for ourselves; wonderfully illustrated by the people we meet. Don't stay where you are tolerated, go where you are celebrated". Learn how to say No! Don't let your mouth overload your back. You'll end up really disappointed if you think people will do for you as you do for them. Not everyone has the same heart as you.

"Make your lifestyle a living testament for others to see and hope to live like you. Our lifestyles should be a living testament for all to see and hope to be like us!". It takes strength to not get offended by the opinions of others. Self Confidence and self worth creates the foundation of that strength. Forgive the past. It is over, learn from it and let go. People are constantly changing and growing. Don't cling to a limited, disconnected negative image of a person in the past. See that person now. Your relationship is always alive and changing.People inspire you or they drain you and pick them wisely. The less you respond, critical, argumentative people, the more peaceful your life will become. Don't try to figure out what other people want to hear from you; figure out what you have to say; it's the one and only thing you have to offer. I have come to realise that the only people I need in my life are the ones who need me in theirs even when I have nothing else to offer but myself. It's not about who is real to your face, it;s about who stays real behind your back.

Some people will only love you as much as they can use your loyalty ends where the benefits stop surrounding yourself with those on the same mission as you if the people you surround yourself with aren't going your way, drop them off where they're going and keep moving full speed ahead. I love people who make me laugh, I honestly think it's the thing most people love to laugh. It cures a multitude of ills. It's probably the most important thing in a person. "Everyone is a teacher. Some I seek, some I subconsciously attract. Often I learn simply by observing others. Some may be completely unaware that I am learning from them, yet I bow deeply in Gratitude." Sometimes it's better to politely excuse yourself from a person's ignorance than entertain them with your intelligence. Don't try to figure out what other people want to hear from you; figure out what you have to say. It's the one and only thing you have to offer.

"Disappointment is coming, for sure! People are going to hurt you in ways you would never have believed even possible. You are going to be let down and deeply betrayed. And there is only one thing to do when you are tragically let down. Let Go! No matter how wrong they were, holding on will not make it right, and it will eat you alive over time. Don't let them kill you twice. Letting go is the only way." You're elevated by others who believe in you!. No matter how good a person you are there will always be someone criticizing you. I am thankful for the nights that turned into morning, friends that turned into family and dreams that turned into reality. To be happy is to appreciate the value of this day, this moment and of those we love who are with us right here and right now. Do what you must and your friends will adjust. Being honest might not get you lots of friends, but it will always get you the right ones. Silence is better than lies. Despite what you may believe, you can disappoint people and still be good enough. You can make mistakes and still be capable and talented. You can let people down and still be worthwhile and deserving of love. Everyone has disappointed someone they care about. Everyone messes up, lets people down and makes mistakes. Not because we're imperfect and fundamentally human. Expecting anything different is setting yourself up for failure.

Being true to yourself means living in truth with each person in your life. It means refusing to say or do something that you don't believe is right. Living in truth with other people means that you refuse to stay in any situation where you are unhappy with the behaviour of another person. You refuse to tolerate it. You refuse to compromise. Don't worry about what others think, just focus on yourself and stay Systematically Positive Always. Some people are always negative, so don't let it bother you. "Stop holding onto people who keep letting go of you. Pay attention to the faithful people. The ones you don't have to impress. The ones who always have your back. The ones that love you with no strings attached." As you move forward in life, you may need to change your circles of friends. Everyone around you isn't interested in seeing you improve. "Once you characterise a man by his actions, you will never be fooled by his words," You can give a person knowledge, but you can't make them think. Some people want to remain fools, only because the truth requires change.

Ten painful truths 1)The average human life is relatively short. 2)You only ever live the life you create for yourself. 3)Being busy does not mean being productive. 4)Some kinder failure occurs before success.5)Thinking and doing are two very different things. 6)You don't have to wait for an apology to forgive. 7)Some people are simply the wrong match for you. 8)It's not other people's job to love you; it's yours. 9)What you own is not who you are. 10)Everything changes, every second. Strong people stand up for themselves, but the strongest people stand up for others to be someone's hero today and everyday.

Donate your time or money. Never be afraid to raise your voice for Honesty and Truth and Compassion, against Injustice and Lying and Greedy Worldly Systems of Control. If people all over the World did this, it would change the Earth's Value Systems. "The worst distance between two people is misunderstanding". I don't trust people who don't love themselves and yet tell me, "I love you". There is an African saying which is; "Be careful when a naked man offers you a shirt". "They see the shine, not the grind. They see the praise, not the pain. They see the money, not the work. They think it's easy, not stressful. They think it's a career, not a calling. They think I Chose it, not that it chose me God!, if they only knew", discover your calling hidden deep inside you.

"Love cannot be found where it doesn't exist there's a difference between being patient with someone and wasting your time". "A man with dreams needs a woman with vision. Her perspective, faith and support will change his reality, if she doesn't challenge you then she is not good for you. Men who want to stay ordinary will tell you not to have expectations of them, men who want to be great will expect you to push them, pray with them and invest in them." "Someone who is worthy of your love will never put you in a situation where you feel you must sacrifice your dignity, your integrity, or yourself worth to be with them." "A woman's loyalty is tested when her man has nothing. A man's loyalty is tested when he has everything." "There is no need to rush, if something is meant to be, it will happen. At the right time, with the right person, for the right reasons". Boys need face-to-face time with good men because they need to see a good man to know how to become one. "Patience is not about how long someone can wait, it's about how well they behaved while they wait". "Don't pick a woman just because she will look good in the team uniform, choose a woman who won't quit the team if you hit a losing streak!." "You love with your heart, but you first lust with your eyes." When you care for someone more than they deserve, you get hurt more than you deserve. Life is about balancing Systems, be kind but don't let people abuse, but don't be deceived. Be content, but never but never stop improving yourself. I just wanna say. Life's too short to worry about stupid things. Have fun, fall in love, regret nothing and don't let people bring you down. Forgive and move on, don't hold on to hate. They hurt you, but you'll hurt even more if you refuse to forgive. Let it go so you can prepare to receive all that you deserve from life. Keep your heart of compassion open.

"It's crazy how you can go for months or years without talking to someone but they still cross your mind every day." "Often it is the same story different person, every person you meet claims to want this or that, but what they really desire is things their way. When it truly comes down to it, the love of the flesh trumps love in the hearts of many. The common courtesy of love, respect and walking together is tossed out of the window. People would rather believe their negative thoughts, fears and opinions of others. Stop claiming, you want love when you have never done anything to really prove you want it." Many are just stuck in the past and keep repeating the same mistakes, if you want a successful relationship love has to be your badge. Physical attractions are common, but a mental connection is rare. Once you have the latter, the former will never be enough.   "A woman's heart must be so hidden in her Godly self, that a man has to seek to Overstand her Godly Systems to find her". A real man never stops trying to show a woman how much she means to him, even after he has got her. "Some of the biggest challenges in relationships come from the fact that most people enter a relationship in order to get something; They're trying to find someone who's going to make them feel good. In reality, the only way a relationship will last is if you see your relationship as a place that you go to give, and not a place you go to take. 10% of conflicts are due to differences in opinion. 90% are due to tone of voice. "A tongue has no bones, but it is strong enough to break a heart. Be careful with your words.

Sometimes the smallest step in the right direction ends up being the biggest step of your life. Tip toe if you must but take that step. "True love is when you touch someone with your Spiritual System, and in return they touch your Soul with their Heart." "Two things to remember in life. Not all scars show, not all wounds heal. Sometimes you can't see the pain someone feels. The most beautiful people, we have known are those who have known defeat; known suffering; known struggle; known loss and have found their way out of the depths. These people have an appreciation, a sensitivity and an understanding of life that fills them with compassion, gentleness and a deep loving concern, beautiful people do not just happen." "Missing someone isn't about how long it has been since you've seen them or the amount of time since you've talked, it's about that very moment when you find yourself doing something and wishing they were right there by your side". "there is a thin line between love and hate, that's for sure. You love a person and then you get to hate them, love is a Mysterious System once you open your heart to someone you are allowing that person to break it which leads to hate." life! is for us to live, love is for us to share and loving your life! is knowing your purpose in life! and pursuing it with all you have." "A man's biggest mistake is giving another man an opportunity to make his woman smile." The most hurtful thing you can say to someone is to say nothing at all. Women are like the police, they can have all the evidence in the world but they still want a confession. A flower does not think of competing against the flower next to it. It just blooms, so just do your thing and bloom.

Follow your heart, but don't forget to take your head with you too. Always tell someone how you feel, because opportunities are lost in the blink of an eye, but regret can last a lifetime. Forgiveness is the best form of love, it takes a strong person to say they're sorry and an even stronger person to forgive. Sometimes being strong and moving on is all you can do. If your relationship has more Systematic Issues than your magazine, you need to cancel your subscription ASAP!. Support those who support you, don't let the people who love you starve because you're trying to feed people who weren't there when you were starving family first. I may not say everything perfectly correct; I may not do everything perfectly right. But if my heart is in the right place, and I am trying my best, then I am ok with that. No one is perfect. Sometimes Life Systems don't want to give you something you want, not because you don't deserve it, but because you deserve more. When it's Right it feels good. When it's Right, there is no battle of the egos. When it's Right you can't wait to be there. When it's Right, the rest of everything that truly Matters falls into place.

"Any woman can spend a man's money; ride in his car, and order off the menu. But only a real woman can help a man achieve his goals in life, support him when he's broke, push him to be successful, shower him with Positive Energy Systems, compliment him on a regular basis and never kick him while he's down. If you find a woman like that, make her your real partner for life." "If another woman steals your man, there's no better revenge than letting her keep him. Real men can't be stolen. Don't cheat in a relationship, if you are not happy then leave. If someone in your life is making you feel worthless: (1) You're not. (2) You're amazing. (3) They don't deserve you. (4) Consider whether you're staying in that relationship. A pretty face gets old. A nice body will change, but a good woman will always be a good woman. Always look in the Soul System of the person you want love. When you live, love and dream with an open heart, all things are possible. When someone loves you, they don't have to say it. You can tell by the way they treat you. You are worthy of all love and all good simply because you are alive!. Everyone comes with baggage, find someone who loves you enough to help you unpack. Just because you're mad at someone doesn't mean you stop loving them. Don't be afraid to take risks, let your heart lead you to. Five secrets to a perfect relationship: 1) it's important to have a man who helps at home and knows how to cook, clean and has a job. 2) It's important to have a man who can make you laugh. 3) It's important to have a man you can trust and wants only you. 4) It's important to have a man who is good in bed and enjoys being with you. 5) It's absolutely vital that these four men don't know each other lol!!!.

Don't go looking for a good woman until you yourself have become a good man. You must meet the requirements of your requirements. Chicks are quick to reject a man who lives with his mother but will jump into bed with a man who lives with his wife and kids in a heartbeat. The worst distance between two people is misunderstanding. Today tell a woman she is beautiful, actually do this every day of your life you will soon meet the love of your life and make many female friends. If you sit quietly with an open heart, it will find you. I hope love finds you as you search for it wherever it may be, it could be the girl next door, or a girl on the internet million miles away. Just keep searching with an honest heart and you will soon find love. You can't hate yourself happy. You can't criticise yourself thin. You can't shame yourself wealthy. Real change begins with self-love and self-care. A wise physician once said, " The best medicine for humans is love? Someone asked "What if it doesn't work?"He smiled and answered "Increase the dose". Be a living, breathing expression of love. There is no need to convince anyone of anything. The most powerful way to teach is by example: A man has done nothing for you until he has made you a wife. Stop idolising boyfriends. The greatest influence you can have in any situation is to be the presence of love. Never ignore a person who loves you, cares for you, and misses you, because one day, you might wake up and realise you lost the moon while counting the stars.

So many go into relationships hoping to get something to make them feel complete. When in actuality, a relationship is about sharing who you already are in your wholeness and then bathing in the beauty and adventure of that!. "If you love two people at the same time, choose the second one, because if you really loved the first one you wouldn't have fallen for the second." "Beauty begins the moment you decide to be yourself. One of the cruellest things you can do to another person is pretend to care about them more than you really do. Every man has two men in him, a king and a fool. How do you know you have found your Queen? When she speaks to the King in you. Ladies, a guy is only insecure about losing his girl when he knows someone else can treat her better. No one can set your level of worthiness except you. You cannot heal what you refuse to first acknowledge."

NOTICE: You are hereby allowed to be happy, to love yourself, to realise your worth, to believe in great things and to be treated with love and respect. Let people love you for who you are, because what you are is more than enough for anyone!. Wisdom integrated with love recognises potentiality and pursues it with a calm passion. Unconditional love patiently waits whether you choose to love unconditionally now or later. When you have love; faith; compassion and hope. You are on your way to a great Systematic life!. Life is short. Don't miss opportunities to spend time with the people that you love. Respect yourself enough to walk away from anything that keeps you from loving yourself. Raise your vibrations, not your voice and not your defences, allow yourself to walk away with peace in your heart. When the power of love overcomes the love of power. The World will know peace. 14 000 people are having sex right now, 25

000 are kissing. 50 000 are hugging and you are reading my book Abundance Now!!!, thank you!

Love isn't when you can name a million things you love about the person. Love is when you can't even find words to describe how you feel about them. "When they discover the centre of the universe, a lot of people will be disappointed they are not it." Remember, anyone can love you when the sun is shining. In the storm is where you learn who truly cares for you. "A wise woman knows the importance of speaking life into her man. If you love him: believe in him, encourage him and be his peace. Nothing like a love that makes you forget that your worries even exist; your heart deserves a love that erases all your problems." You'll never be enough to somebody who can't recognise your worth. You can't make them see what they choose to stay blind to. Letting go doesn't mean you forget the person completely, it just means that you find a way of surviving without them. The funny thing about a strong woman is that she doesn't need you. She wants you. And if you start slacking she'll be content without you. "Never expect, Never assume, Never ask, Never demand. Just let it be. If it's meant to be it will happen." No one knows your situation better than you. Do what's best for you and explain it to them later. If they can't love you through it, they weren't meant to be in your life. Be with someone who is proud to have you. Relationships Systems last longer when nobody knows your business!

Always believe something wonderful is going to happen. Even with all the ups and downs, never take a day for granted. Smile, cherish the little things and remember to hug the ones you really love. "You'd never invite a thief into your house. So why would you allow thoughts that steal your joy to make themselves at home in your mind?" When we detach from our need to hold on, we allow the beauty of our reality to unfold through love. Learning to appreciate every little thing about you, allow yourself to love yourself all the time, even when you screw up which is pretty often. Spend life with people who make you happy, not whom you have to impress. "Negative people don't always occur as negative to me. I like to think of their Systematic Negativity as unfinished and when I can, I love them without labelling them as Negative. Because "Darkness cannot drive out darkness: only light can do that, Hate! cannot drive out hate: only love! can do that."

A woman with a beautiful body is good for a night, but a woman with a beautiful mind is good for a lifetime. A relationship without trust is like a car without fuel. You stay in it all you want, but it won't go anywhere. You might think she wants your car, your cash and gifts. But the right woman wants your time, your smile, your honesty, your efforts and you choosing to put her as a priority. Keep your thoughts positive because your thoughts become your words. Keep your words positive because your words become your behaviour. Keep your Behaviour positive because your behaviour becomes your habits. Your habits become your Value Systems, so keep your values positive because your values become your Destiny. Your past never has to equal your future, unless you let it. Be yourself, be honest, do your best. Take care of your family. Treat people with respect. Be a good citizen. Always chase your dreams. Self-belief Systems are the Strongest Magic. Doubt kills more dreams than failure ever will.

When you are no longer ruled by worries about what others think of you, you become free to be yourself. Go as far as you can see when you get there, you will be able to see farther. To make the right choices in life, you have to get in touch with your soul. To do this you need to experience solitude, which most people are afraid of, because in the silence you hear the truth and know the solutions. Challenges create change, and change promotes Growth!. Know that every challenge has an expiration date! No matter how long the night, Day follows!.

Sometimes you need to look back, just to find where you dropped your standards. Lost your confidence and started settling for less, than you deserve. Once you discover that place, pick them back up, make peace with that time in your life and march on with your head held high. Sometimes when we feel so alone and beat down it's when God steps in to rebuild and mold us into who we are destined to be. "Dear God if today I lose my hope, please remind me that your plans are better than my dreams." God will always make a way when there seems to be no way. Just because you got a little older doesn't mean you got a little less amazing. In fact with age you have become more wonderful, more beautiful, more dazzling. Never forget, your best years are ahead of you!!!Instead of being discouraged by opposition, be encouraged by it. Knowing that on the other side of that difficulty is a new level of your destiny. As iron sharpens iron, your difficulties are going to sharpen you. This is your time, this is your moment. You are being equipped, empowered and anointed. "No weapon formed against you can prosper". As we express our gratitude, we must never forget that the highest appreciation is not to utter words, but to live by them. "Never reply when you are angry, never make a promise when you are happy." Never make a decision when you are sad.

Don't downgrade your dreams to match your reality, Upgrade your faith to match your destiny. As I stated earlier "Sometimes all you need is a hundred million dollars don't we?" You'll never know what you're capable of until you take that first step and go for it. Sometimes letting things go is an act of far greater power than defending or hanging on. "Always reach and strive for the next level and never settle for less than your very best" "Ask for what you want and be prepared to get it!". Don't lose heart now keep going you are much closer than you think. "Only put off what until tomorrow what you are willing to die having left undone" Believe it can be done. When you believe something can be done, really believe in it in your mind you will find a way to do it. Believing a solution exists paving the way to the problem. Watch your thoughts, for they become words.

I was born in Soweto South Africa in my Granddad's house. I was born at 6.05 on Easter Sunday 29th March 1970, the Star Systems must have been well aligned as I have had a very Enlightening Life which I will share with you now. My Mother's family are Moyo who have Royal Systematic Connections originating from Bulawayo in Zimbabwe and my Father's family Mnisi was originally from Swaziland the original Royal's for the Swazi people. The Mnisi Kingdom is currently situated in South Africa. At the age of six as I was starting my primary in 1976 in Pimville Winnie Ngwekazi Primary in Soweto, in June 1976 the students in Soweto Uprising began to strike against being taught in Afrikaans instead of English. I was caught up in the mayhem as I recall being chased by Police Hippo trucks and dodging bullets as I ran home to find my father waiting for me. It was decided that night that I had to leave South Africa to get a proper education in Swaziland where I went for a couple of months and then it was Rhodesia (Zimbabwe) which was undergoing an intense guerrilla warfare waged by the Zipra forces under Joshua Nkomo. I first attended Saint Bernard's Primary School in Pumula and then I was enrolled in a Multiracial Catholic Boarding school Sacred Heart Bush-Stick primary where I got my indoctrination from. This school was closely guarded by the Rhodesian Army and I recall one incident when we were fishing and we were confronted by some guerrilla forces who threatened to kill all the whites kids if I didn't get them some food from the Nun's. I recall that incident like it happened yesterday, and from that day we were banned from fishing and we got a lecture from the Rhodesian Army soldiers.

In 1977 I was only 7 years old then, I flew from Bulawayo to Johannesburg for the first time by myself for School holidays to Jan Smuts Airport in South Africa I was so terrified. On our train journey back to school my mother decided to take my twin brothers Sipho and Sipihwe with her aged 4 years. What happened at Mafikeng still amazes my Mum and me today. We got stopped from crossing the border to Zimbabwe because my twin brother Sipihwe who suffered from some medical ailments from birth and didn't have the correct medical certification to cross over so we had to get it in the morning. The black police officer at the border even offered us his dining room floor to sleep. After all that hassle only to find out that my brother's health certificate just saved our entire family as our compartment was bazookered that night. I was shocked to actually see the coach lying on it's side and seeing the big black hole in our previous compartment as we passed it the next day and that made me wonder how much God has played an important part in our lives and still seems to always be there during my trying times and joyous times too.

Aged 9 in 1979 my mum arranged for me to travel ahead of her to Harare where I was housed by my Mum's aunty Mrs Mundawarara my Gogo who was married to then Vice Prime Minister Dr Mundawarara R.I.P you are surely missed Khulu, at that time Abel Muzorewa was Acting Prime Minister of Zimbabwe/Rhodesia. I recall meeting both and chatting to them aged nine.

In 1980, I was 10 years old when my Mother came to Harare where she enrolled me into David Livingstone school. I am just glad to attend the Bob Marley Concert and got to dance with him on stage Google Redemption Song Harare 1980 I am the crazy kid dressed in brown, I was soon shipped off to boarding school again in 1981 this time Godfrey Huggins Primary where I learnt how to dream. I got to meet Joshua Nkomo in 1981 through my mother and in 1985 aged 15 while we attended the Bulawayo Trade Fair he came up to me and asked me how my mother was? I got to know him and I visited him on his deathbed in 1999 during a visit to Harare R.I.P Mudlala Wethu. Aged eleven in 1981 I lived in my head half the time until I was woken up by my chosen high school Allan Wilson A-Dub aged 15 years in 1985 now that was a wake up call from my day-dreaming of self-actualisation. Allan Wilson was good for me because it taught me how to become a man, and it has instilled certain self achieving sporting codes which I still use today. I became an all round sportsman playing Rugby, Gymnastics, Cross Country Running, Swimming, Tennis, Hockey, Cricket and Waterpolo making it the School teams in my age groups every term.

In 1987 I moved Churchill Boys High School which was another adventure as I just sailed through it, and created a War Cry which is now being used by most schools in Zimbabwe now "Churchill Here we Go! In the Sun, in the rain, no sweat! no pain! not yet!"I was sponsored by World University Services (W.U.S) of Canada through Themba Ndaba who helped me register my brothers too. Imagine in 1987 aged 17 until I became 21 in 1991 I was paid Z$1000+ every month for attending school. In 1991 after a big 21st Birthday party that lasted three whole days in the rain too. We as a family repatriated back to South Africa using the United Nations scheme. In 1992 I enrolled myself into the Association of Advertising Agencies School of Advertising in Johannesburg which I later changed to Cape Town, I was at this time being sponsored by the ANC. I met loads of people and dealt Marijuana from my flat in Senator Towers by Long Street. My flat had the view of Table Mountain. Imagine waking up every morning and being woken up by Table Mountain. It was great for two years.

This when I felt Like met the devil as I was being tempted into his world because I started dealing in Cocaine and Malawian Marijuana Cobs making loads of fast cash which was spent just as quickly too. I felt an evil presence around me which I couldn't shake off like it wanted to gobble me up, I decided to headed to GrahamsTown Art Festival in 1992 a place where knew I could sell off my Malawi Cobs as I had loads to sell, I made my first sale quite quick and the word got around that I had the best stuff. Then things started happening in Grahamstown that I can only explain now after 25 years after the incident it now makes sense. I was arrested in Grahamstown because I had long dreadlocks because they never found anything on me and the police kept calling some guy God in front of me and he never showed his face to me. I questioned the police why they were calling a person God on earth and they couldn't answer me.

They locked me up after a humiliating bath and radiation exposure as they left me in a room with Nuclear warnings signs around, then they took me to my cell where I saw this man made of light and I lost my marbles because I felt like that police cell was like Hell about to let loose and I couldn't stand being in that cell. I was kept in it the despite my loud cries for help as I went through what I call a transformation when I saw that old man made of light with long white hair my heart cooled me off and I accepted the light as he never spoke a word but held out his hand towards me in a jester and from that point I knew I was going to beat this and I lost my marbles really went mental. They took me their local mental institute where I believe I met the devil disguised as a mental patient as it was staffed by white people and this guy kept questioning me about things I was yet to do, which scared me because he spoke in riddles and would tease me and never let me sleep for three whole nights until my Mum came and then he suddenly disappeared.

My Mum became my strength as she brought me freshly cooked meals and advised me not take their pills as they force fed us tablets. After three days I came around my Mother says as I was like in a haze before, my mum could tell that the old Vinny was back slightly and she took me back to Cape Town a broken man having fought a Spiritual battle. I was welcomed back by my then girlfriend Claudia Klaase and now ex-wife, who agreed to look after me while I recovered as my Mum had to go back to Zimbabwe. When I got to my flat I wrote pen to paper for three whole days. None stop not even for food and sleep. I wrote about all the evils of the White Supremacy especially about their history in Witchcraft, Wars, Slavery and Apartheid. I wrote about the future too which I cannot recall. I am sad to have lost that work which I tried to revive in writing Africa Must Unite in 2010 which was kinder off raw as some white friends here in the UK told me that I sounded angry. I toned it down to The United Countries of Africa Now!!! in 2012.

In 1995 I got employed by Hunt Lascaris TBWA after another battle, I had applied to them using ANC letterheads and since they handled the ANC Advertising account I felt they were obliged to hire a student who was sponsored by the ANC. After waiting for 3 months and my calls being ignored I cut my dreadlocks and went to their Offices in Sandton, only to be given a Letter of Appointment and Ken Modise resigning from a Directorship position to make room for me. Imagine that I go to confront them on why they have not replied to me and they answered me by giving me a Letter of Appointment. I signed it and immediately went cloth shopping at Edgars on credit.

1995 was a turning point, I was twenty five years old and hungry to learn and I did learn indeed firstly under the Account Directorship of Lyn Mausenbaum a Jewish lady that taught me loads about the functionalities of an Advertising Agency and how we handled clients with kids' cloves. She taught me all I know and still use today, I can only be thankful to her. She properly introduced me to Nelson Mandela at the ANC office after I had met him at a Rally I had organised in Kwa-Zulu Natal, I recall meeting Aunty Joyce at the ANC Shell House Office and she was shocked to see me in a suit waiting in her office about to meet up with Nelson Mandela the next President of South Africa.

I actually first met Nelson Mandela in Durban in KwaZulu Natal where I had arranged an ANC rally which was attended by Mandela and Jacob Zuma he came up to me and shook my hands both hands and said "So you are Vincent Mnisi" I replied "Yes Sir" and he replied "You are doing good work for us" and I replied "Thank you sir." I was actually shocked that he knew my name beforehand. I went to his house Houghton to record his voice too. I got to spend a little time with him may his soul rest in peace. How I met Jacob Zuma is another situation as before the Rally I had to do a reiki of the venue and advise them on security details. I stopped the metro rail from operating because it rode just above the stadium and since there was friction between Inkatha and the ANC. I thought that Inkatha would deploy spinners on the Metro Train and they could shoot from it. Zuma called me into his ANC office in Durban and said to me in Zulu "Hay young man why do you want to stop the rail" I answered in Zulu ``Because I am worried about being shot by a stray bullet from the metro I have a lot to live for" he answered "I see young man go back your hotel". What happened at that event still amazes me because the Inkatha began shooting into the stadium from outside causing commotion and stamped. We had to get Mandela out via helicopter and we, my white Director and I had to drive out of there.

In which I took control of the private hired car and shouted in Zulu with fist pumps while my director covered her white face with a black scarf and I just drove past their roadblocks without stopping. I am just glad we survived that, South Africa is a beautiful country run by evil people. This is a place where you can get hijacked and robbed in broad daylight at gunpoint. I met Cyril Ramaphosa too the current President when he came to sign the cheques at the Hunts AMC offices he seemed sceptic of me because he gave me uncomfortable looks, you must recall I forced my way into Hunts after threatening them with media exposure for not hiring me as student who had been sponsored by the ANC into advertising and they handled millions of rands worth of advertising from the ANC.

I was attacked by people I didn't know and by people I knew from birth even now I feel South Africa is still fighting the evil spirits off Apartheid. I have been back in 2015, 2017 and 2019 after 14 years of self imposed exile because I wanted my daughter to have the best access to uplifting herself. On my trips back I felt like the youth are still being misled and miseducated and it will take time to uplift the masses from extreme poverty. Education is the key to self actualisation. Free education for all in South Africa until Doctorate level must be accessible to those who want to learn. In 1995 was the year I met the South African World Cup winning Rugby too at the final as I was in Mandela's entourage as it was my Job to make sure he engaged it the right public events at AMC Hunt Lascaris TBWA.

I worked for Hunts for two years winning them millions of Rands of Advertising revenue on the fact that they had me as black face and they were only paying me R3500 per month as a Trainee Account Executive which they raised to R6.500 after I had a word with the Finance Manager. I was then offered a job doubling my salary in 1997 by Adactive Advertising, a small hotshop doing the CNA Stores advertising. I jumped at the job offer after showing my Manager the offer letter and listening to her advice to take the job. My work at Adactive dried after I had a tragic accident in which I needed plastic surgery on my face three months later. Claudia and I decided to move to Cape Town after being tipped off a possible job by Ken Modise after a chance meeting at a Shopping centre in Sandton. I went to Cape Town to join Young and Rubicam Advertising as their Research Officer for Gilbeys Liquor Brands and GoodYear Tyers. This when my drinking became bad, I recall my ex-wife advising that I needed the AAA. I went to one meeting.

I was still dating Claudia Klaase who became my wife in 1997 after a quick court marriage and the Mother of my only daughter Lyndiwe who was born on the 15th of July in 1997 at Groote's Schcree Hospital in Cape Town. I eventually settled down into AWSG JWT as an Account Manager for the Nike advertising account, I enjoyed it but it got very strenuous with the flying twice sometimes three times weekly flights to Johannesburg I soon accumulated some Air Miles which I used to visit The Mnisi Royal Dam Swaziland in 1998.

In 1999 I left AWSG JWT because of the China Kids Nike scandal that had broken up and I joined P4 Radio as their Strategic Planner writing out Advertising proposals for their sales department. I then got bored at P4 Radio and was asked to join another venture, an Investment Company which I undertook with an American Medical Doctor Derrick Hubbard. I even worked on a business plan in which my mum got funding to start a Hair Salon from Barclays Bank South Africa when it existed. The venture failed because of some cheque discrepancies that occurred at the office.

I became a Jobless alcoholic and ran out of money to live on. I turned to a friend who started supplying me 10 kilos of Swazi Marijuana every week which lasted for six months ending badly because everybody got greedy and in that business once you get greedy someone gets hurt I am just glad that I never got hurt as they threatened to kill my daughter and eventually I did get burnt like my supplier bypassing me to the buyer after I had introduced them big mistake. My ex-wife had to get a job at Pizza place for the first time since we had been together from 1991. I moved back to Johannesburg in 2000 only to get a job in two weeks working for MTN paying me R18 000. I was then offered a job by 8 Seconds Advertising to join them as an Account Manager for their MTN account which I took up as it was paying R32000 per month and they needed me too. I had a stroke two months after joining 8Seconds Advertising

After my stroke 8 Seconds Advertising decided to let me go after paying me off with R96 000 which was three months salary. I decided to recuperate at my Mum's house in Bulawayo in Zimbabwe, the stroke had affected my short term and long term memory. I couldn't remember anything even what someone just said or what I just watched. I was like a zombie. At least my daughter was living with my mother, as she looked after her for us aged six months while Claudia was attending the AAA School of Advertising being paid for by my Mother. I enjoyed the time I spent with my daughter then because it rekindled my spirits and I regained myself again.

In 2002 my brother Sipho travelled to the UK. We both took the leap of faith and we both now have Indefinite Leave to Remain in the UK granted in 2002. I then got a job working 5 night 12 hr shifts and earned about £300+ per week at Pride valley Foods for 4 years. I was then sending my Mother and Daugther weekly transmits. After a phone call which I still recall today when I sent my mum money she told me "Vincent you didn't go England to work find a university and study" which I did four years later after I had enrolled into Manchester Metropolitan University, I then sent my Mother and Daughter money to come an join us in 2006. I now recall I had an impromptu speech in front of my Advertising class at Manchester Metropolitan University, I was helping a coughing lecture explain the workings of an Advertising Agency and since I had worked in Advertising before I felt obliged to help her out. After speaking from my heart and not even using her notes my own classmates gave me a standing ovation, asking for my phone number and if I could help with this and that. I was surprised by their reaction and I am always led back to that day as it was my first taste of public speaking. After my stroke in 2000 I got really addicted to Alcohol as it became a coping mechanism for me and I was drunk half the time, I even wonder how I kept passing.

I soon moved back to the University of Sunderland in 2007 to finish my Degree which I topped up with Business Management element to my Advertising and Brand Management from Manchester Metropolitan University. My drinking got worse. I would go for days without taking a bath and just drank cider Scrumpy Jacks from morning to night time. I recall meeting Kudzi in one of my lectures after I had not attended a single class for months and he was surprised to confirm that we shared a lecture. My Mum intervened again and sent me to a Christian rehab at the Victory OutReach in Manchester where I compiled my first proper book "Africa Must Unite". Which I later revised to "The United Countries of Africa Now!!!" I cannot thank my mother enough as she has never given up on me as I had a couple of relapses since and she even took me to see T.B Joshua in Nigeria in 2015 in her attempts to make me teetotal. I recall leaving rehab for three days in 2010 so that I could Graduate which shocked my rehab housemates, even the staff from the JobCentre were all surprised to see me in my Graduation Gown as they had always seen me walking around town drunk or half drunk.

I became totally teetotal in January 2017 after a final warning from the Misters at the Manchester Royal Infirmary, for the first time in 20 odd years of drinking daily I have finally stopped drinking for Now! I can feel it in my bones?. "I don't need a drink" I have also written nine books, This one been my ninth. Thanks to Kudzian Micah Munogi for reading it, for the encouragement to pursue this writing project and for always being a driving force in all my endeavours in also pushing me to accomplish my Masters in Marketing Communications in 2018. My family includes my Mum Busi Elizabeth Mnisi "The Queen", my brothers Sipho Louis Mnisi and Siphiwe Lois Mnisi R.I.P I miss you plenty my Brother, and my one and only daughter Lyndiwe. My friends George Morris and James Zwandaziwah who nicknamed me "Chiyangwa" and I hope you have been inspired and motivated to accomplish those goals and dreams you have been shelving for years. I would like to also thank Lawrence Davis from New York City for the afterword.

It's now time to start doing and stop talking about your hopes to people until it is done, something that I also need to learn to do myself too. Peace and Love to you all and thank you for reading Life! I hope you have been inspired by it. Have a splendid day, week and life! "Learn to enjoy every minute of your life, be happy now, don't wait for something outside yourself to make you happy in the future. Give so much time to the improvement of yourself that you have no time to criticise others, live in faith that the world is on your side for as long as you are true to the best that is in you." "Revive your light, manifest your dreams, realise your worth, the most important thing is to realise yourself worth. When you know your worth, you set standards for you. Don't be pushed by your problems, be led by your dreams." "Once you connect with yourself it is impossible to be lonely or desperate for other peoples company. Be Happy like my name sake, Be Bright, Be You! The distance between your dreams and reality is called action…Go forward in life with a twinkle in your eye and a smile on your face always with great strong purpose in your heart. I advise you all to watch David Icke's interview with Credo Mutwa. He confirms that the Europeans used witchcraft to subdue Africa and the World, I must warn you it's a six hours long watch. I will summarise with somes quotes from my African Unity books "Africa Must Unite", "The United Countries of Africa Now!!!" With also some quotes from my third book "Inspires Aspire for Assertiveness" And my seventh book "The Afrikan Spiritual Bible"…

"Africa Must Unite because of the common history and social conditions Africa's share, our societies have been more inclined to take for granted the Europeans desirable models, the thoughts as well as the artifacts of the dominant colonial culture. Artifacts indeed which we cannot do without such as Electricity; Cars; Telephones; Television; Western Music and European Literature etc. We can adopt all these but we will only become mimics if we do not adopt them fully conscious of our own History, Culture and Traditions." "Africa needs to establish its own think tanks and Social Institutions. Africa needs to cultivate upon our music and arts. African Hip Hop is making trends worldwide become creative, create yourself out of poverty by self discovery and selling yourself to the world". "We must adopt a critical attitude both to what we have and what is brought to us. This should be a guiding principle in the selection of what we teach and how we teach it.

African writers the creators of new Literature need to give us in this area of critical thinking." "Our aims of teaching our youth should be to produce men and women who are both critical and creative. Our students should be encouraged to be thinkers and doers rather than accumulators of facts and received knowledge. It's time to start seeking knowledge from within. I am the future, we are the Future, let's build a stable African society without any striving and want ``"This must be so if they are to be instrumental to the change that is needed. African Youth need to communicate with each other and one African universal Language must be adopted by the African Union, which must be taught at every school in Africa. This Must be so if Africa aims to start working towards the realisation of a just and consequently stable African Society.

African Spirituality is simple and does not require you to attend a church, you are the church. Firstly you have to overstand your heritage and speak to your families from both sides. Mother and Father get to know your family history and rediscover your true worth on earth. Always listen to that inner voice, your intuition, it's your Godly Spirit talking to you listen. I will quote Emperor Haile Selassie. I the last King of Ethiopia "Spirituality does not come from religion. It comes from our soul. We must stop confusing religion and spirituality. Religion is a set of rules, regulations and rituals created by humans, which was supposed to help people grow spiritually. Due to human imperfection, religion has become corrupt, political, divisive and a tool for power struggle. Spirituality is not theology or ideology. It is simply a way of life, pure and original as was given by the Most High of Creation. Spirituality is a network linking us to the Most High, the universe and each other"......By Haile Selassie I "God is in all and He encompasses all...This is the secret of life: Man lives in God and God lives in man. This answers all questions"... Those who turn away from the glorious jewel within to seek an outside god, a separate, unresponsive being, are looking for a mere trinket, while disregarding the priceless treasure already in their keeping"....Kolbrin Bible Download it's for free now and get enlightened, deep I must say!!! hopefully resonates with your soul....."Man worships, not to make God greater, for this he cannot do, but to make himself greater. Nothing man can do can add to what God already has. Men conceive God as a Being having greatly magnified human qualities, as a kinglike Being greater than any king. Thus man falls into error... "Among earthly things man shall find nothing greater than himself. God is in all and He encompasses all. ...Kolbrin Bible

"A lifting hand is worth ten wagging tongues. Be a man of fortitude and courage. Prepare to fight, for Earth gives man but two choices: to struggle or perish. There is work to be done in the Garden of God, therefore cease useless performances and word-wasting discussions, go, pick up the hoe and tackle the task at hand"... "If a man would know Heaven, he must first know Earth. Man cannot understand Heaven until he understands Earth. He cannot understand God until he understands himself, and he cannot know love unless he has been loveless. God is unknown but not unknowable. He is unseen but not unseeable. God is unheard but not unhearable. He is not understood but He is understandable. The goal of life is upstream, not downstream. Man must struggle against the current, not drift with the flow. A child is born knowing all God intended it to know, the rest it must discover for itself. Man does not live to increase the glory of God, this cannot be done, but to increase the glory of man"....Kolbrin Bible

"The purpose of all human life is a goal so glorious it surpasses all earthly understanding. We may visualise our individual goals as we will, it is ordained that we have this freedom. How close or how far we are from reality is of little consequence, what is, is. He who seeks a non-existent destination will, nevertheless, get somewhere. He who seeks not at all will get nowhere. Earthly life fulfils itself without attainment".....Kolbrin Bible

"Man sees glory by the reflected light of glory within him, he knows love by the love within himself. The sun is seen by the light of the sun and not by any light within man. Man sees the spirit by the light of the spirit, and not by any light within his mortal self. Only by the light of the spirit can the spirit of man be lit".... "I am the living consciousness within you, I am the knower. The things seen by the eye and the things smelt by the nose are received by me. The things heard and the things felt are registered by me. I am the inner being causing all decisions to be made, though the tongue reports back outside the things that I, the soul and the spirit, hold recorded. Everything done and undertaken, such as the working of the hands and movement of the legs, all are done in accordance with my command"....Kolbrin Bible

"Men reap as they sow and I am the Fertile Field which takes no part in the sowing or the reaping. Man is his own master and the lord of his own destiny. He cannot expect help from any great power, unless he himself expands effort to contact such power or be deserving of help. Everything a man is or becomes is the result of his own striving and efforts, or his lack of them. I made a man to be a man",... "I am not influenced by the mere formal actions of men, or by empty sacrifice. Lighted lamps and candles, days of fasting and self-mortification by man cannot sway Me in his favour. I am not to be bribed, for I am God....Kolbrin Bible

I am the God Who ordained the Law, and nothing man can do will change it. My love alone mitigates the consequences of man's unredeemed wickedness."...Kolbrin Bible

"I am the Changeless One. Could a God of Love become a God of Vengeance? Revenge is something alien to Me. Therefore, is it reasonable that men should believe I could be one thing today and then because they fall into error and become something else tomorrow? My nature is not that of man. I AM as I AM......Kolbrin Bible

Wherever there is a human begin, there is an opportunity for kindness...by Seneca

Great things are done by a series of small things brought together...by Vincent Van Gogh "Living with integrity means: Not settling for less than what you know you deserve in your relationships. Asking for what you want and need from others. Speaking your truth, even though it might create conflict or tension. Behaving in ways that are in harmony with your personal values. Making choices based on what you believe, and not what others believe... By Barbara De Angelis. Be daring, be different, be impractical, be anything that will assert integrity of purpose and imaginative vision against the playitsafers, the creatures of the commonplace, the slaves of the ordinary...By Cecil Beaton. Killian F Bukutu a good friend wrote this "Never wait for the perfect moment, use the moment and make it perfect....Just because the past didn't turn out like you wanted it to, doesn't mean your future can't be better than you ever imagined...

LIFE IS AMAZING AND I AM GLAD THAT I WAS BORN TO LIVE MY LIFE AS I HAVE BEEN TRULY BLESSED!!!!!!!!!.....THANKS YOU ANCESTORS AND GOD FOR ALL YOUR THE GRACE AND ACKNOWLEDGEMENT.
I ONLY HAVE YOU TO THANK FOR ALL MY OPPORTUNITIES THAT YOU SEEM TO ALWAYS SHOWER ME WITH THANKS AGAIN....AMEN

RESPECT YOURSELF ENOUGH TO WALK AWAY FROM ANYTHING THAT NO LONGER SERVES YOU, GROWS YOU, OR MAKES YOU HAPPY...By Vincent Happy Mnisi But Don't let a single Moment of Misunderstanding be poisonous; That it Makes Us forget the hundreds of Lovable Moments spent together! Never leave a TRUE Relationship for a few Faults, Think just once, Nobody is Perfect, Nobody is always correct and at the END, Affection is Always Greater Than Perfection......Unknown..

LOVE CANNOT BE FOUND WHERE IT DOESN'T EXIST. THERE'S A DIFFERENCE BETWEEN BEING PATIENT WITH SOMEONE AND WASTING YOUR TIME, THERE IS NO NEED TO RUSH LOVE, IF SOMETHING IS MEANT TO BE, IT WILL HAPPEN, IN THE RIGHT TIME, WITH THE RIGHT PERSON FOR THE RIGHT REASON AND IF FEELS RIGHT IT WILL NEVER GO WRONG, UNLESS YOU LET IT.....By Vincent Happy Mnisi.

A MAN WITH DREAMS NEEDS A WOMAN WITH VISION. HER PERSPECTIVE, FAITH AND SUPPORT WILL CHANGE HIS REALITY, IF SHE DOESN'T CHALLENGE YOU THEN SHE'S NO GOOD FOR YOU. MEN WHO WANT TO STAY ORDINARY WILL TELL YOU NOT TO HAVE EXPECTATIONS OF THEM, MEN WHO WANT TO BE GREAT WILL EXPECT YOU TO PUSH THEM PRAY WITH THEM AND INVEST IN THEM........UNKNOWN

PROVERBS 27:1 DO NOT BOAST ABOUT TOMORROW, FOR YOU DO NOT KNOW WHAT A DAY MAY BRING FORTH...

The power of Thoughts
Thoughts are very powerful, thoughts are illustrations of the mind that have either constructive or destructive possibilities over our emotions. Occasionally there are imaginations as imaginations are pictures that occur to you through your thoughts which can occupy one in bondage or set you free. Until you change a man's thinking you cannot change his life, the swiftest means to change your life is by altering your manner of thinking..until you change your thinking you can't change your life..your current state is your making from your past thoughts, your present circumstances was made by your past thoughts renew your mind be reflective of your thought as most thoughts are negative, start thinking positive..you and only you are responsible for your life, you are the builder and breaker of your life. The mind is so powerful, it works with what you feed it. Feed your mind with positive thoughts constantly, plant remarkable qualities in your mind, don't just dwell in life without projecting on harvesting in your mind. You need to develop into and manifest upon your thoughts in your mind....By Vincent Happy Mnisi..

If we ever stop thinking about the person we want to become, we stop learning and taking risks...by Sally Blount

Don't wait for compliments from people, learn to compliment yourself daily because only you know the good work that you are doing...Be a Chance, take a chance and be like me you will get somewhere instead of thinking about it, just do it...Lay hold of your destiny, declare your future and demand it. Renew your thinking by exchanging your thoughts of defeat, negativity, weakness and adopt thoughts of strength, victory and overwhelming prosperity. Success is measured at different levels of life and you can hit success upon success as it is unlimitless...By Vincent Happy Mnisi

Africa needs to invest in educating our youth for free to University level and nurturing our woman; children and old folk from Cape to Cairo.My aim is to mobilise the African Community to combine their Gross Domestic Product (GDP) and to form one currency, economic integration which will benefit all Africans. Africa Must Unite because of the common history and social conditions which African countries share, our societies have been more inclined to take for granted as most desirable models, the thoughts as well as the artefacts of the dominant colonial culture. Artefacts indeed which we cannot do without: Electricity; Cars; Telephones; Television; Western Music and Literature etc. We can adopt all these but we will be only mimics if we do not adopt them fully conscious of our own History; Culture and Traditions. Africa needs to establish our own Social Institutions and cultivate upon our music and our arts. We must adopt a critical attitude both to what we have and what is brought to us. This should be a guiding principle in the selection of what we teach and how we teach it. African writers and the creators of the new literature need to give us a lead into this area of critical thinking. Our aims of teaching our youth should be to produce men and women who are both critical and creative. Our students should be encouraged to be thinkers and doers rather than accumulators of facts and received knowledge. This must be so if they are to be instruments of change, working towards the realisation of a just and consequently, stable AFRICAN SOCIETY....Africa needs to unite NOW!!! economically at least we need to form a United Gross Domestic Product (GDP) in-order for Africa to form one currency which will compete against the Euro; £ and the USA$ in the world markets because Africa holds most of the natural resources the world needs today. Africa has a rich cultural heritage of UBUNTU, we Africans need to socialize in order to grow in the arts and music. We have to start setting targets to achieve Millennium Development Goals which will fulfill African Societies aims.

Africa Must Unite Economically for the betterment of its people in-order to consolidate Africa's natural resources. I feel like I am meant to do this and that God has been preparing me for my destiny and I am very grateful only to God and my family for my life which I love very much! very!! very!!!MUCH!!!...I pray that my short and long term ambitions get fulfilled as I undergo accomplishing things day by day. I thank GOD and My Ancestors as I carry my African Royal Spirit and Glory wherever I go. I embrace my Ancestral Heritages as they bestow a life of wonder and overstanding my purpose on earth. I am here to enlighten mankind from the European deceptive miseducation as its weapon of psychological warfare on the African mind. Christianity is mental warfare against the African mind time to wake the fuck up from the indoctrinations that come with being Christian. Wake Up Africans please?I must say that I live a simple life here in England, I don't work but write full time for my company which the Job Centre helped me form and they pay me £600 a month until I get a breakthrough with one book which may never happen at least not now as our African people are still asleep sad but they don't want to read?!?

"There is no passion to be found playing small in settling for a life that is less than the one you are capable of living"....By Nelson Mandela this quote has made me think about my own situation and circumstances and I am thankful for my current situation as I have benefited from living the life in England, I enjoy it as I have been writing books for the last 10 years and I can only be grateful to God and my Ancestors for the inspirations and the motivation to accomplish every book venture...I must say that I am thankful to the UK as it has allowed me to accomplish all my hopes and dreams of first attaining a Degree in Advertising and Business Management which I obtained from Manchester Metropolitan University and then a top-up Business Management Degree from The University of Sunderland...and then My Masters in Marketing Communications which I have just accomplished in 2018 at Manchester Metropolitan University.

There thing is that after living here for over 18 years...the only place where I see myself fulfilling my ambitions and fulfilling my destiny is in Africa...I hope and want to get into politics in the next 5-10 years time and my ambitions are to be part of the group of African Leaders that will finally Unite Africa...Help set up an African National Social Services Africa (ANSS)(UBUNTU) a robust Social Service to be branded (UBUNTU) in the same element as the European Union Countries have for their populations. Africa needs to invest in educating our youth for free to University level and nurturing our woman; children and old folk from Cape to Cairo.My aim is to mobilise the African Community to combine their Gross Domestic Product (GDP) and to form one currency, economic integration which will benefit all Africans. Africa Must Unite because of the common history and social conditions which African countries share, our societies have been more inclined to take for granted as most desirable models, the thoughts as well as the artefacts of the dominant colonial culture. Artefacts indeed which we cannot do without: Electricity; Cars; Telephones; Television; Western Music and Literature etc... We can adopt all these but we will be only mimics if we do not adopt them fully conscious of our own History; Culture and Traditions.

Africa needs to establish our own Social Institutions and cultivate upon our music and our arts. We must adopt a critical attitude both to what we have and what is brought to us. This should be a guiding principle in the selection of what we teach and how we teach it. African writers and the creators of the new literature need to give us a lead into this area of critical thinking. Our aims of teaching our youth should be to produce men and women who are both critical and creative. Our students should be encouraged to be thinkers and doers rather than accumulators of facts and received knowledge. This must be so if they are to be instruments of change, working towards the realisation of a just and consequently, stable AFRICAN SOCIETY....Africa needs to unite NOW!!! economically at least we need to form a United Gross Domestic Product (GDP) in-order for Africa to form one currency which will compete against the Euro; £ and the USA$ in the world markets because Africa holds most of the natural resources the world needs today. Africa has a rich cultural heritage of UBUNTU, we Africans need to socialize in order to grow in the arts and music.

We have to start setting targets to achieve Millennium Development Goals which will fulfill African Societies aims. Africa Must Unite for the betterment of its people in-order to consolidate Africa's natural resources. I feel like I am meant to do this and that God has been preparing me for my destiny and I am very grateful only to God and my family for my life which I love very much! very!! very!!!MUCH!!!...I pray that my short and long term ambitions get fulfilled as I undergo accomplishing things day by day...Thanks GOD!!!!!!!!!!!!!!!!!!!!!!!!!!!..

Religions were established to enslave the mentality of mankind to believe in an outside source for salvation when they should be looking inside of themselves for their own eternal salvation as you only save yourself no one is coming to save you but you and your senses...Time for African Governments to stop stealing the taxes and start spreading them amongst their populations which will be good for the producers of goods too...Time to wake up Africans...Time to demand you're right share to your Countries Taxes you have shares too your Birth Certificate is proof of share ownership to the Republic Tax Systems you were born in which is listed on the stock exchange...Time to wake up Africans time to demand monthly payments from your Governments if you are out of work like they have it here in Europe and everywhere in the first world...Africa is been made into a 3rd World and that's not right we Africans should be living like Kings with the amount of mineral wealth we are born with....Time for Afrika to Awaken!!!..

I have been writing for the African Market for 10 years now and I have probably only sold 100 to 200 books in total from my 8 books. Sad but true and I will not stop as my work will be appreciated by the next generation not this brainwashed one.....Simple lifestyle is the way to go.. I am glad, I slowed down from the Advertising Executive Lifestyle mode of live fast and die young, my early years where fast and grand too life is what you make it and all you need is a bed and food really...Happy Holidays everyone don't drink to much as you are killing yourselves slowly wish I had known that ten years ago. Europeans have used deep psychology to take over the African Minds. They can't own land in Africa like they originated from there? The Queen and the French too, not forgetting The Church of England and the Roman Catholic Church own acres of land all over Africa…

Our Gold and Diamonds are still owned by Europeans. How come? land Rights should be abolished for all foreigners in Africa ASAP!!! In this book Abundance it looked into Capitalism as it's a predatory system of life and my thoughts are now thinking of Europeans as evil beings for establishing such an evil system of living... I have come to that conclusion that they are an strange race and they aim is to rape Earth for all its got. As stated before my thoughts for Abundance have taken me into weird spheres of thoughts because why did they establish a system which is going to be manipulative at every point from Education, Business and Religion? Is my question and even teaches it in schools how to manipulate the markets and cheat the consumer... They have planned everything for centuries.. Like All Countries are part of the Capitalistic systems listed on New York and London Stock exchanges...we have to break this Predatory Social Economic System of Governance ASAP!!!

People born with Gold and Diamonds on the soles of their feet shouldn't be made to starve and beg for food predatory Capitalism is humans shouldn't have to need money to survive. This economic system in place is unworkable without a start-up for humankind. We have to overhaul everything and install a Human Economic System. Public administration should be transformed into a process of self-governance within political and economic institutions based on assumptions of generative rather than degenerative principles that replace fear with love, scarcity with abundance, self-interest with mutual interest, and dialectical competition and hierarchy with collaboration.

Abundance seems to elude the rich and the poor alike. For some, too little money leads to unhappiness. For others, too much money complicates life in unwanted ways. Regardless of how much money comes into our lives, after our basic needs are met, an increase in income tends to lead itself to increased consumption. Somehow, a treadmill effect ensues, and often whatever accoutrements we do have are never quite enough. Fortunately, spiritual happiness depends neither on abject poverty nor on material success. Spiritual happiness is cultivated in places where money and material possessions have no dominion. It is from this place that we can discover the truth of what it means to live in a state of abundance...Unknown

"Peace upon Mankind of goodwill and purpose, for the World belongs to them" By Vincent Happy Mnisi

Abundance Summary

This book is written to awaken the Entire World especially Africans from the deceptions of Christianty, Capitalism, Stock Exchanges, Currency Exchanges and that the Private ownership of mineral resources should be done away with as soon as possible. The Debeers and the Anglo Americans have got no rightful ownership of the Diamonds and the Gold that they mine as those minerals belong to all Mankind. This Capliatisc World we live in now is systematically set to benefit Europe and undying profitable Companies whose main purpose is to amass as much profit from the public that it's meant to serve. Profit should not be the aim for companies, every company's aim is to break even and making profits should be just a bonus because your product or services are being well received by the public. The business practices Elasticity of Demand and by creating scarcity when there is enough Gold and Diamonds to fulfill everyone's dreams. The Earth's Wealth must be shared by its citizens. With the technologies in place soon the need for human labour will soon be obsolete. Open design technologies will enable customers to be involved in the creation or customisation of their goods they want in a way not seen before and reverses the trend of people simply being passive consumers. Citizens of the post-scarcity society are encouraged to pursue higher education with the aim of learning essential life skills, skills one needs to make the most out of life as proposed by Raul Prebich which will become essential tools for the way forward.

In the paper by Professor Maitreesh Ghatak which provided the conceptual overview of an alternative mechanisms that leads to poverty traps at the individual level, he made a distinction between those that are due to external frictions (e.g., market failure), and those that are due to behavior under extreme scarcity in the absence of any frictions. The Population factor will play an important role as they will create a world of divine happiness and total wealth for everyone on earth with free capital injections for every human viable venture. I propose a World Government with equal rights for all Mankind, no more divisions on nationalities but Citizenship of the World or Race. The World must move away from the divide and rule and conquer ways of the past and stop wars which are caused by the division. The arms race must stop and wars must be stopped too. What is the purpose of Nuclear Armament in the first place? Stock Exchanges and other Manipulative Institutions must be closed and the World should start dealing in one currency which can be made digital as everyone has a mobile phone and every Human Being must get some form of monthly payment from the World Government and Capital assistance for Home Building and for Businesses ventures too…

This current CoronaVirus 2020 World Health Crisis has brought about self isolations and workers who are able to work from home are being encouraged to do so. My personal opinion on this virus is that it's man-made to eradicate human populations worldwide as AI is now ready to take over human labour and is their way of using the Devilish New World Order Totalitarian Government. I personally believe that this Coronavirus is another man made Biological Technological Weapon let out through their 5G rollout try to reduce the World Population so stay as warm as possible as it can not live in hot temperatures and always keep your hands disinfected. There is certain speculation on social media that this CoronaVirus epidemic is being caused by the implementation of the new 5G network roll out hence they want us to stay indoors while they roll it out. While we have been under struct lockdown measures, concerned citizens have found 5G Antenna been mounted overnight in the dark of the night and the amount of radiation emitted from them has also been measured too by a member of the public using his own radiation reader which reached the dangerous levels for human and animals too. One person captures dying birds and animals close to freshly mounted 5G Antennas.

I hope this book has opened up your third eye of consciousness to the real realities of the World we live in now, I think it's time for a change don't you? It is time to build a New World Order with new ideals and to move away from wars, chasing paper money and from the divisions that we have created through Nationalities, Religions and Cultures which creates Wars. It's time to adopt a New World Order where everyone belongs to one World Citizenship…I hope this book is not mistaken for pushing for the New World Agenda 2021/30 programme it's actually an opposition to their propositions of extreme human control. Humans should be free and must be free to do whatever they feel like doing with no limitations or control. I feel this virus is serving as an introduction of what is yet to come "Total Control of Human Movements" be warned!...Dr Nina Fedoroff the former Science and Technology advisor to the US once stated "We need to decrease the growth rate of the global population; the planet cannot support many people" which I can second guess this means killing people purposely or stopping the birth rate through abortion programmes. Google The Rockefeller Foundation Scenarios for the Future of Technology and International Development written in 2010 which created a similar we are experiencing now with this current CoronaVirus on page 18 LockStep describes a similar lockdown and total abuse of human right ad how convenient and conciencitedantil that Bill Gates the founder and manufacturers of the CoronaVirus Vaccine thinks of creating Event201 where billions of people gets a Corona Viral diseases transferred from pigs in Brazil. Check the it Youtube the enacted this event in September 2019 giving the population the kind of harm the world will come to. This current crisis is claimed to come from bats in an animal market in China as claimed by mainstream media, I am still keeping an open mind about things and hopefully life will come back to normality soon….This CoronaVirus is like a bad April Fools joke that won't go away!

This social distancing is getting to me and it's affecting people too as it's making people scared to interact. In 1975, Henry Kissinger established a policy-planning group in the U.S. State Department's Office of Population Affairs. The depopulation "GLOBAL 2000" document for President Jimmy Carter was prepared. It is no surprise that this policy was established under President Carter with help from Kissinger and Brzezinski all with ties to David Rockefeller. The Bush family, the Harriman family the Wall   Street business partners of Bush in financing Hitler and the Rockefeller family are the elite of the American eugenics movement. Even Prince Philip husband to the current Queen of England is also member of The Bilderberg Group is in favour of a depopulations programme and once stated "If I were reincarnated I would wish to be returned to earth as a killer virus to lower human population levels" Prince Philip Duke of Edinburgh, leader of the World Wildlife Fund, quoted in "Are You Ready for Our New Age Future?" Insiders Report, American Policy Center, December 1995. Speaking at a gala event in London recently, the Duke of Cambridge Prince William the future King of England said overpopulation is destroying the planet. Stating Prince William stated that in order to save flora and fauna the planet should be depopulated. Prince William recently warned that the population growth in Africa is putting a tremendous amount of pressure on the natural world and driving many species of animals to extinction. He stated "Africa's rapidly growing human population is predicted to more than double by 2050 a staggering increase of three and a half million people per month," Prince William explained during a recent event hosted by the Tusk Trust, a charity that is committed to protecting African wildlife. "There is no question that this increase puts wildlife and habitat under enormous pressure." I rest my case now it's up to you to make your own assessment with the evidence I have just provided. Peace be with you and upon the world too...I hope this book has enlightened you!.....

"Limitations are like mirages created by your own mind. When you realise that limitation do not exist, those around you will also feel it and allow you inside their space"...By Stephen Richards

Thee World Bank Economic Review Advance Access published April 16, 2015 by Professor Maitreesh Ghatak

Theories of Poverty Traps and Anti-Poverty Policies

In this paper by Professor Maitreesh Ghatak which I felt needed to be included in this book Abundance Now!!!This paper provided a conceptual overview of alternative mechanisms that lead to poverty traps at the individual level, he made a distinction between those that are due to external frictions (e.g., market failure), and those that are due to behavior under extreme scarcity in the absence of any frictions. Maitreesh Ghatak developed a common theoretical framework to examine alternative scenarios, characterizing conditions under which poverty traps (in the sense of multiple stable steady states) arise, as opposed to (possibly, conditional) convergence to a unique steady state. He applied this framework to discuss the relative merits of alternative anti-poverty policies, such as unconditional and conditional cash transfers, and direct interventions aimed at improving market access to the poor or improving public service delivery. I have added or subtracted any content from this paper in

INTRODUCTION

There are two distinct strands of thinking on poverty. One view is that the poor are just like the nonpoor in terms of their potential (that includes ability, preferences), and they simply operate in a more adverse environment, in terms of individual characteristics (e.g., factor endowments) or economy-wide characteristics (e.g., prices, infrastructure, various government policies). The best known statement of this view is Schultz's phrase "poor but rational." Modern development economics has extended this view to what Duflo (2006) calls "poor but neoclassical" by studying various frictions that impede the smooth functioning of markets as well as technological nonconvexities that make it disadvantageous to be poor or operating at very low scales. We lump these together and call them "external frictions" (along with frictions that arise from poor governance, infrastructure, etc.) that prevent the poor from making the best use of their endowments through exchanges in the marketplace or through technology.

THE WORLD BANK ECONOMIC REVIEW, Published by Oxford University Press on behalf of the International Bank for Reconstruction and Development / THE WORLD BANK. The World Bank Economic Review Advance Access published April 16, 2015 by Professor Maitreesh Ghatak

The implicit premise of this view is that poverty is a consequence of individuals operating with an unfavorable external environment. To the extent this can be fixed by placing a poor individual in a more favorable external environment, it will be a transient phenomenon but otherwise the poor may be trapped in poverty. In a sense, in this view the phenomenon of poverty, other than being inequitable, is also inefficient: a combination of individual rationality and market forces should work to utilize any potential gains (e.g., lost income from insufficient investment in human capital) and the question is, what external frictions prevent this from happening. Avery different view of poverty is, even if there were no external frictions, the poor are subject to different pressures and constraints from the nonpoor and that drives them into making choices that are very different, and more importantly, that can reinforce poverty. Having very low incomes means an individual has to engage in a day-to-day struggle for survival for herself and her family, and there may be a self-reinforcing dynamics at work through the choices that are made under extreme scarcity that keep those with poor initial endowments of financial and human capital, poor over time and across generations. It is tempting to call this view "poor but behavioral," but we are going to argue that this is a broader phenomenon, as even if all individuals are rational in the neoclassical sense, choices under extreme scarcity can reinforce the tendency of the poor to stay poor. For example, at very low income levels, subsistence considerations may rule out the feasibility of saving at a reasonable rate, and investing money in health and education to secure a better future for themselves and their children. In fact, the relevant scarce resource does not have to be money but can also be time or attention span.1 In this paper we develop a conceptual framework and simple unifying model that distinguishes between what we call "friction-driven" and "scarcity-driven" poverty traps corresponding to the two views of poverty discussed above. We start with a standard dynamic model of an individual saving or leaving as bequests a constant fraction of income, and investing over time and study how her income and wealth grows. Then we introduce various external frictions and study conditions under which rather than converging to a unique steady state, there could be multiple stable steady states, and which steady state an individual ends up depends on her initial wealth, that is, a poverty trap exists. We focus on poverty traps at the level of individuals and adopt a partial equilibrium approach (i.e., take prices as given) to examine under what conditions two individuals who are identical in all respects but only differ in their initial wealth may end up with different steady state wealth levels. We do not look at aggregate or macro level poverty traps, where interest rates or wages adjust with capital accumulation.

1. See Banerjee and Mullainathan (2008) for a formalization, and also Mullainathan and Shafir (2013) for various examples.general equilibrium effects.2 We then extend the model to relax the assumption that people save a constant fraction of their income and allow the choice of saving to depend on income in a non proportional way (which results from non homothetic preferences) and characterize conditions for poverty traps to emerge. We consider the role of behavioral biases as well as insufficient intergenerational altruism in this context. We draw a number of interesting inferences. We show that capital markets frictions play an important role in determining the possibility of poverty traps, but these are neither necessary nor sufficient for poverty traps to arise, even if we restrict attention to friction-driven poverty traps. This suggests being careful in making inferences about whether poverty traps do or do not exist from any piece of evidence suggesting the presence or absence of any single friction. We also show that poverty traps can exist even without any external frictions due to the operation of strong income effects in the behavior of individuals, and this is possible without any behavioral biases.

We then discuss the distinctive policy implications of these two kinds of poverty traps. We will focus on a representative "poor" agent and assume that the policymaker has some resources (which are costly due to taxes being distortionary and there being alternative uses of public funds) and wants to help the poor individual escape poverty, defined in terms of some minimum level of income, consumption, or wealth. For the most part, we assume the policymaker's objective function is the same as the individual's preferences, but in some cases there may be grounds for having paternalistic preferences. We distinguish between policies that are aimed at improving market access to the poor as well as improving productivity in general (e.g., through better public service delivery) by dealing directly with the frictions and those that involve direct transfers to the poor. We show that for both types of poverty traps, lump-sum transfers work (under some conditions). However, if poverty traps are friction-driven, then it is possible to substitute lump-sum transfers with "supply side" policies that directly tackle the frictions. We also show that to the extent scarcity and frictions coexist, there are strong complementarities between policies that increase the purchasing power of the poor and those that are aimed at removing a friction. We show that to the extent the preferences of the individual differ from that of the policymaker (which can be due to behavioral biases or insufficient intergenerational altruism or gender bias), unconditional lump sum transfers will not be the most efficient form of intervention and there may be a case for "paternalistic" interventions such as conditional cash transfers. The plan of the paper is as follows. In the next section we develop a benchmark model without any frictions, as well as any scope for the behavior of the poor to be different due to the operation of income effects. In the third section

2. See Azariadis (1996) and Banerjee (2003) for reviews of the literature on poverty traps. See Mookherjee and Ray (2003) for an example of a poverty trap with general

equilibrium effects that arise from the equilibrium returns from different occupations adjusting in response to individual choices.

Professor Maitreesh Ghatak analyzed poverty traps that are driven by frictions (subsection titled External Frictions) and choice under scarcity (subsection titled Non-Homothetic Preferences). In the fourth section we discuss the policy implications of our theoretical framework. The final section concludes with some observations of interesting issues that are worth exploring further in future research.

THE BENCHMARK MODEL

In this section, we develop a standard model of a representative individual using capital to produce output, with no market friction or any kind of nonconvexity. In addition, we assume preferences are homothetic in income, and therefore, in a proportional sense, there is no difference in the "behavior" or "choices" of the poor from that of the rich, say, in the context of savings. One-Period Model Suppose production (q) depends on one input (x) given by a standard neoclassical production function:

q ¼ AfðxÞ:

A denotes the productivity parameter which could be driven by skills, ability, infrastructure, institutions. The function f(x) is assumed to have the standard properties of a neoclassical production function. Whenever convenient, we will use the example of the Cobb-Douglas production function: q ¼ Ax a where a [ð0;1Þ. We will focus here on physical or financial capital, denoted by k and so x¼k. We will consider the role of other inputs in the next section. Here we can think of a self-employed individual using capital to run a business. To keep the notation simple, we assume k is working capital and therefore, fully depreciates after use. Since capital fully depreciates with use, returns to a unit of capital, denoted by r, has to exceed 1: That is, r is the gross rate of interest. As mentioned earlier, we focus at a representative individual, and take r as exogenously given all through. An individual has capital endowment k. Her profits are p

ient level of nutrition. The higher wages that would result form being more productive would help them pay off the loan. To get a poverty trap in this setting, one would need capital markets to be imperfect. Other Market Frictions Let us augment the basic one-period model of section 2 by adding an additional input, h, which we will refer to as human capital (but can be interpreted as other inputs such as land i¼max k

AfðkÞrk: With perfect capital markets her income is: y ; p þr k:

This shows that the endowment of capital or wealth does not matter for productive efficiency although it does matter for final disposable income. Through rental or sales (in a one-period model they are equivalent), they adjust to maximize efficiency, with all production units using the same amount of capital given by k* which is a solution to Af0ðkÞ¼r. If someone is capital-rich, she can lend capital, and borrow otherwise.

Therefore, with perfect markets and no frictions (e.g., nonconvexities), we have a separation between productive efficiency and individual economic outcomes.3 To the extent we care about an individual's income falling below some minimum threshold, that is, poverty, there is a case for redistributive transfers, but they will not have any positive productivity impact on the recipient. Infinite Horizon Model We now introduce dynamics in the one-period model to allow for savings and capital accumulation over time so that the current endowment of the capital stock k (equivalent to wealth in this model) is the result of past choices rather than being exogenously given. We assume preferences are homothetic and people save at a constant rate s, as in the Solow model. Alternatively, we can assume that individuals live for one period, pass on a constant fraction s of their wealth as bequests to the next generation. In the next section we will examine the consequences of relaxing the assumption of a constant saving rate. The constant rate of saving or bequest can be micro-founded in the following way that is standard in the occupational choice literature (see Banerjee 2003). Suppose individuals have preferences over consumption (c) and bequests (b) and the utility function is given by: Uðc;bÞ¼logcþ b logb where b 0. As is standard, we assume bequests cannot be negative. If we maximize this subject to the budget constraint cþb y then we get the usual result: b¼sy where s ; b 1þ b . This budget constraint implies the presence of intertemporal borrowing constraints. We will discuss the implications of this assumption, as well as that of bequests being non-negative later in this section. Let kt denote the capital endowment in time t. The bequest of generation t determines capital endowment in period tþ1:bt ¼ ktþ1. With perfect capital markets we get: ktþ1 ¼ sð p þrktÞ:

Assuming sr , 1 we get convergence to a unique steady state as figure 1 shows, using a familiar diagram. In the figure, the grey line (we will turn to the concave curve in the next section) represents the equation that gives the evolution of the capital stock over time. The unique steady state capital stock k is given by k ¼ s p 1sr

:3. This is the same as the separation result in the context of Agricultural Household Models, as developed by Singh, Squire, and Strauss (1986). Since we assume no interpersonal heterogeneity, all individuals will converge to the same steady state k, that is, we have unconditional convergence. However, as is well known, convergence may take time depending on parameter values, and so as in the one-period model, there may be a case for pro-poor policies on redistributive or equity grounds.

DE PA R T U R E S F RO M BENCHMARK MODEL

Now we proceed to study two sets of departures from this model: first, we introduce external frictions that constrain the choices available to the individual, due to market imperfections, technological nonconvexities; second, we look at the consequences of individuals having non-homothetic preferences, so that the poor behave or make choices that are different from those who are not poor even in the complete absence of external frictions.

External Frictions

In this section we discuss relaxing various assumptions of the model outlined in the previous section that allow the possibility that two individuals who are identical in all respects except for their initial endowment of capital (or wealth), k0, can end up with different levels of incomes and capital stocks in steady state, which is a formal way of describing a poverty trap in this framework.

Below we discuss the consequences of relaxing a number of assumptions in the benchmark model. Capital Market Imperfections Suppose capital markets are imperfect. In fact, for expositional simplicity, let us assume that there are no capital markets. This means, on top of intertemporal borrowing constraints, it is not possible to borrow to finance working capital within a given period. In the one-period model the separation result breaks down: output is now q ¼ Afð kÞ. Turning to the infinite-horizon model, the case of no capital markets is equivalent to the standard Solow model where individuals save a constant fraction of their income to accumulate capital over time. As we assume capital fully depreciates, the modified transition equation is: ktþ1 ¼ sAfðktÞ:

This is captured by the concave curve in figure 1. Following a standard argument, there will be convergence to k, assuming r is given by the marginal product of capital evaluated at the steady state capital stock, namely, Af0ðð̃kÞ.4 Initial conditions will not matter in the long-run. Of course, if A differs across individuals then we get conditional convergence. What this diagram shows is, if we introduce capital markets, convergence is speeded up. The capital stock used in production will reach the steady state level right away, while the owned capital stock of the individual will grow along with income, and eventually reach this steady state level. We could allow intermediate levels of capital market imperfections, where the amount of capital that an individual can use is some multiple of her initial capital stock, i.e., s k0 where s . 1 (and not too large so that capital market frictions do have bite), which can be generated by one of the standard channels of credit market frictions, such as ex ante or ex post moral hazard (see, e.g., Banerjee 2003). The main lesson of this exercise is that, subject to the same fundamentals, being capital-poor is no handicap in the long run as individuals accumulate and converge to the same steady state even if capital markets are imperfect. Of course, the convergence can take a long time and this might be grounds to have in place policies that facilitate access to capital of the poor. But history does not matter, and one-shot policies cannot have long term effects: two individuals who are identical except for their initial endowments of capital being different will end up in the same steady state. However, if there are additional frictions, then capital market frictions can lead to poverty traps, as we will see below.

4. This is in order to have the same benchmark under these two different scenarios (perfect and no capital markets), and can be justified by the assumption of having many atomistic individuals with the same deep parameters (A, s etc), but with different initial

values of k0 (and in particular, those with k0 k being able to meet the demand of those with k0 , k, on aggregate).

Nonconvexities Suppose the production technology is subject to nonconvexities. In particular, let us introduce set-up costs as an example of nonconvexities in the following form: q ¼ AfðkÞ; for k k ¼ w;otherwise: where 0 w , Af ðkÞ, is returns from a subsistence activity. It is assumed that the subsistence activity needs no capital and only labor. It is possible to interpret this nonconvexity as reflecting imperfections in the market for some input other than capital. For example, suppose without a minimum amount of land, production using the modern technology (given by Af(k)) cannot take place. Clearly rental markets or time-sharing arrangements could overcome this indivisibility and to the extent those are not possible due to some institutional or contracting friction, the indivisibility will have bite. At the end of this section we will explore the role of inputs other than capital and imperfections in those markets. First let us assume capital markets are perfect. Then profit maximization yields p ¼ max k AfðkÞrk for all individuals since the subsistence technology is an inferior option. As a result, with perfect capital markets the equation of motion is:

ktþ1 ¼ sð p þrktÞ for all k 0: As before, we will have a unique steady state at k ¼ k. Therefore, with perfect capital markets, an individual can borrow k or more, and so the indivisibility does not bind and there is no poverty trap. If capital markets are absent then the transition equation is given by: ktþ1 ¼ sAfðktÞ for k k ¼ sðwþktÞ; otherwise:

Since the subsistence activity needs no capital, any capital that an individual owns is part of total income, but there is no interest earned on it, as capital markets are assumed to be absent. We are assuming that saving is feasible even without capital markets, for example, through some storage technology. Also, we are assuming that all individuals save a fraction s of their income whether they are operating the subsistence technology (for which no capital is needed) or the modern technology. We could alternatively have assumed that for k k individuals don't save at all, that is, ktþ1 ¼ 0 and that would not change our conclusions. We postpone the discussion of the saving rate varying with income to section 3.2. For k k, the transition equation is strictly concave and increasing as in the case of no nonconvexities and autarchy. This part is depicted by the concave curve in figure 2. Fork k, the transition equation is linear, as given by the transition equation above. As there are no capital markets, the transition equation has slope s rather than sr. It is depicted by the thick and grey line segment in figure 2. As we can see that there will be multiple steady states: for those whose initial endowment of capital was k or more will converge to k H while those who started with less than k will converge to k L , k H. This is an example of a poverty trap: initial conditions matter, even in the very long run. However, having capital market frictions and nonconvexities is not sufficient for poverty traps. If s or w are high enough (as depicted by the dashed line segment),then it's possible to save one's way out of the poverty trap.

5 Even if the production technology is convex, nonconvexities can arise in other ways. For example, suppose A (which captures complementary inputs, such as, infrastructure) depends on k such that wealthy get an advantage, that is, A¼ A(k) and in addition, this function is subject to nonconvexities. If capital markets are perfect, then individuals should be able to overcome this indivisibility through borrowing. A similar argument applies if in the absence of capital markets that prevent borrowing or saving through external financial institutions, the poor in addition, do not have access to a good savings technology (e.g., storage), due to, say, imperfect property rights while the rich do (because, e.g., it is easier to steal from the poor). To the extent the relationship between wealth and the effective savings rate (as opposed the intended one, which is determined by preferences) is subject to nonconvexities, poverty traps can result.

5. Non-convexities can take many other forms (e.g., an S-shaped production function that captures increasing returns at low levels of capital, and diminishing returns at higher levels in a more continuous way), but the basic intuition of our analysis goes through.

Alternatively, suppose that if c c, people do not survive or are unproductive (similar to the nutrition-based efficiency wage argument as in Dasgupta and Ray 1986). Now the transition equation is

ktþ1 ¼ sAfðktÞ for ð1sÞfðktÞc ¼ 0; otherwise: Again, we will get a threshold k defined by the equation ð1sÞfðktÞ¼c:

If capital markets are perfect, individuals can borrow to and invest in their health and therefore, there is no poverty trap. Otherwise, this form of nonconvexity, like those for the production technology, the savings technology, or the productivity parameter A, can generate poverty traps when coupled with capital market imperfections.6 More broadly, even though we have taken here the example of physical capital, the point about the relationship between capital market frictions and nonconvexities affecting the production technology applies more generally. Instead of a minimum consumption constraint, suppose the productivity of individuals depend on nutrition (as in Dasgupta and Ray 1986) and that relationship involves nonconvexities. If capital markets existed and were perfect (a possibility that Dasgupta and Ray [1986] do not allow), individuals would have borrowed and achieved the efficn some contexts, as discussed below). Suppose the initial endowment of human capital of the individual is h and that h can be obtained from a competitive market at cost r per unit. Output is now q ¼ Afðk;hÞ:Profits are p ¼ qrk r h. Profit-maximization yields the standard first-order Conditions: fkðk;hÞ¼r fhðk;hÞ¼ r :

6. An alternative way of treating minimum consumption constraints is discussed in the next section, where people choose to save at a lower rate when they are poor. Here it is modeled similar to an external biological constraint like "maintaining" the (human) capital stock.

The optimal levels of ^ k and ^ h can be solved from these as functions of r and r and as before, the endowment of the individual will not matter in determining productive efficiency, although it will matter for the income of the individual. A rental or sales market will achieve the efficient allocation and in the absence of specific contracting frictions, these are equivalent. Even if there is a cash-in-advance constraint that applies for inputs other than capital - namely, they must be paid for in advance in cash - our conclusion is unchanged so long as capital markets are perfect. Now let us assume that there is no market for h (with or without cash-in-advance) while the market for k operates just as before. In that case, the individual's choice of k will be give by: fkðk; hÞ¼r and the optimal choice, which we will denote by ^ k, will depend on h. For convenience, let us assume the Cobb-Douglas production function: q ¼ Ak a h b with a , b [ð0;1Þ and a þ b 1. In this case, solving the above equation explicitly for k as a function of r and h we get ^ k ¼ A a rh b 1 1 a and substituting in the production function, we get q ¼ A 1 1 a a r a 1 a h b 1 a :Net output (taking into account the cost of k) is: q rk ¼ A 1 1 a a r a 1 a ð1 a Þh b 1 a :Let f ðhÞ; A 1 1 a a r a 1 a ð1 a Þh b 1 a

denote net output as a function of h. It is an increasing and strictly concave function of h for the case of decreasing returns ð a þ b , 1Þ or linear in the case of constant returns ð a þ b ¼ 1Þ. Now the individual's income y is net output plus interest earned on owned capital:y ¼ f ðhÞþr k: Turning to dynamics, let ht and kt denote the human and physical capital endowment of the individual at time t. Income at time t is given by yt ¼ f ðhtÞþrkt: The equation of motion for kt is: ktþ1 ¼ sð f ðhtÞþrktÞ for all k 0:

Now we turn to the interesting question, namely, how does ht evolve over time. Suppose income can saved and spent on investing in h, similar to how savings is used to accumulate k. Even though in a given period, h cannot be rented or bought to be used in production, suppose it can be "produced" for the next period by saving a certain fraction of income (e.g., investing in the education of children). In particular, let htþ1 ¼ g y ¼ g ð f ðhtÞþrktÞ where g [ð0;1Þ and sþ g , 1 to ensure that total saving (in k and h) as a fraction of income is less than 1. The advantage of this formulation is that the accumulation equation for h is identical to that for k, up to a multiplicative constant: htþ1 ¼ g s ktþ1: The equation of motion of k in this case is: ktþ1 ¼ sf g s kt þrkt : This allows us to characterize the steady state level of k by standard arguments: k ¼ s f g s k 1sr and h too converges to h ¼ g s k: What is interesting to note is that we do not get poverty traps but unconditional convergence. Of course, this conclusion changes if there are nonconvexities in the relationship between h and y.

Suppose the production function is q ¼ Ak a for h ^ h ¼ Ak a ;otherwise where ^ h . 0 and A . A . 0. The only change from above is now net output as a function of h as captured by f ðhÞis no longer a smooth and continuous strictly concave function but has a discrete jump at h ¼ ^ h. Income y is given by: yt ¼ðAÞ 1 1 a a r a 1 a ð1 a Þþrkt for h ^ h ¼ðAÞ 1 1 a a r a 1 a ð1 a Þþrkt otherwise: Since htþ1 ¼ g yt and ktþ1 ¼syt, both the human and physical capital transition equations will be piecewise linear with discrete jumps at ht ¼ ^ h and kt ¼ s g ^ h, respectively. The transition equation for h is given by:htþ1 ¼ g A 1 1 aa r a 1 a ð1a Þþ sr ghtwith A taking the values A or A, depending on whether ht ^ h or ht , ^ h. There will be a parallel transition equation for k. By standard arguments, we may have two stable steady states, i.e. a poverty trap may exist as we depict in figure 3 (ignoring the dashed grey line for the moment).

Human Capital & Poverty Traps

We have depicted the poverty trap in terms of h, i.e., the long run level of y and h depend on the initial level of h. However, since k depends on income y, the long-run level of k depends on the initial level of h, although not the initial level of k unlike in the earlier model with k being the only input. As noted in the context of a single input production technology earlier, market frictions and nonconvexities are necessary but not sufficient for poverty traps. That would depend on parameter values. Here too if the values of A and/ or sr g are not too low, it is possible that through their saving behavior, individuals escape the poverty trap. If the transition equation for ht , ^ h is given by the dashed line instead of the continuous one, then there is a unique steady-state and that involves a high level human capital in steady state. Let us examine what assumptions drive this kind of a poverty trap. We already saw that when the relationship between h and y was given by a smooth strictly concave function we get a unique steady-state, exactly as in the Solow model. Therefore, nonconvexity in the production technology with respect to h is playing a key role here. It is interesting to think about what is the role of market frictions here. We are assuming capital markets are perfect as far as k is concerned. It can be bought, sold, rented and accumulated without any friction (within a period). The market for h is imperfect however, and that is clearly driving the results. If h could be bought or rented without any constraints, we would get unconditional convergence as we saw above. When h can only be autarchically "produced" by saving out of current output, this reflects a market failure that prevents individuals who have a higher endowment of human capital from transmitting it to children of families where parents have a lower endowment of human capital, e.g., through a perfect market for education. Alternatively, if h is interpreted as land and not human capital, the presumption is, a land-poor individual cannot rent or lease land due to some institutional failure but it is possible to accumulate it through saving out of current income and buying it. However, capital market frictions implicitly show up, in the form of restrictions on intertemporal transfers since what can be accumulated through savings can presumably be bought by a loan. We now turn to this issue.

Restrictions on Intertemporal Transfers There is a sense in which we are assuming an intertemporal capital market imperfection when discussing technological nonconvexities in physical or human capital. Since saving out of income does help accumulate h or k, in principle, individuals could be forward looking, and as capital markets are being assumed to be perfect, they should be able to borrow and/or save at temporarily high rates to get over the hump at ^ h. We briefly explore here the consequences of modifying our basic model of choice between consumption and bequests introduced earlier by allowing individuals to be forward-looking and flexible in their savings behavior and given this, examine the role of intertemporal constraints on resource allocation Suppose as in our basic model output depends on one nonlabor input x given by the same production function q¼Af(x). However, now x is required to be

invested in the previous period to be of productive use in the current period. After use, it depreciates completely. In the current period, individuals are endowed with an exogenous level x0 of x and rental markets are not useful given the lagged nature of the production process. Therefore, current output is q0 ¼ Afðx0Þ, in the next period output is, q1 ¼ Afðx1Þwhere x1 is chosen by the individual at time t¼0, and so on. We can view x as physical or human capital, although the particular lag structure is more suggestive of human capital. If we first think of a two-period model, where in the first-period the individual chooses how much to consume in the present period (c0) and the next (c1), and also how much to invest in x. The individual maximizes logc0 þ b logc1 subject to the intertemporal budget constraint: c0 þ c1 r þx1 q0 þ Afðx1Þ r :

It follows immediately that independent of their preferences over present and future consumption, individuals will choose x1 to maximize their lifetime resources. This is an extension of the separation result mentioned in the one-period model at the beginning of this section to a two-period setting—with perfect markets and no constraints on intertemporal transfers, individual preferences should not affect the efficiency of intertemporal resource allocation. The optimality condition for the choice of x1 is Af0ðx1Þ¼r

which is, the marginal return from investment should be equal to the interest rate. The result holds even if the production technology is non convex with respect to x. Suppose investment is a binary decision x [f0;1g and the cost of investment is normalized to 1. Without investment, output is q but with investment, it is qþD. This is similar to the model with human capital in the previous subsection. So long as D . r individuals would undertake the investment. However, if there are constraints on intertemporal resource allocation, then this property will no longer hold. In the extreme case, it is not possible to borrow at all, and therefore, the budget constraint facing the individual in the current period is: c0 þx1 q0 while in the next period it is c1 Afðx1Þ: The choice of x will now be determined by the condition: 1 c0 ¼ b 1 c1Af0ðx1Þ and x will depend on, among other things, q0 which is determined by the initial endowment of x.

The basic logic extends to the case of individuals with Barro-Becker altruistic preferences, which by a standard recursive argument becomes equivalent to an individual maximizing the present discounted value of the utility stream of current and future generations in a forward-looking way overan infinite-horizon: X 1 t¼0 b t lnðctÞ with an intertemporal budget constraint (using standard arguments to rule out unlimited long-term asset or debt accumulation): X 1 t¼0 ct rt þX 1 t¼0 xtþ1 rtþ1 q0 þX 1 t¼0 Afðxtþ1Þ rtþ1 :

In the absence of any intertemporal borrowing constraints, investment decisions will be efficient, while in their presence, the initial endowment of x will affect investment decisions, opening up the possibility of poverty traps (e.g., if in addition, there are indivisibilities in the production technology). Even if capital markets are perfect as such, in most societies negative bequests are not permissible by law and violations of this are considered morally offensive, such as bonded labor. This is equivalent to an intertemporal borrowing constraint: a poor parent cannot borrow to send her child to school such that the child will pay off the loan when she is an adult. What this discussion implies is that, to the extent bequests are required to be non-negative, this puts a constraint on intertemporal resource allocation which is separate from what is often meant by capital market frictions, namely, constraints on short-term loans. Coupled with other frictions (e.g., nonconvexities in the production technology), this can lead to poverty traps. Of course, additional capital market frictions (due to standard frictions such as problems of enforcement and informational asymmetries) will reinforce this tendency. These could be for short-term loans or for long-term loans, with the latter contributing to intertemporal borrowing constraints. Friction-Driven Poverty Traps - The Key Implications The key points from our discussion of friction-driven poverty traps are as follows. First, no single friction is sufficient to trap individuals in poverty. Whether it is capital market frictions or restrictions on intertemporal resource allocation as

implied by the constraint that bequests have to be non-negative, we would require some other friction, such as non-convexities in the production or the savings technology, to prevent the poor to be able to save the "right" amount of physical or human capital and for their families to escape poverty in the long-run. Therefore, the fact that some studies fail to find any direct evidence of lumpiness of investments alone is not sufficient to conclude that there is limited empirical support in favor of poverty traps. Poverty traps could still result if there are borrowing constraints in addition to lumpiness with respect to the savings technology or in the production technology with respect to some input other than capital. Similarly, the fact that some studies find that microfinance loans have not been effective in reducing poverty significantly too is not conclusive evidence against the presence of poverty traps. First of all, without the "right" amount of loan it may be hard to escape the trap. Also, to the extent there are indivisibilities in the production technology with respect to other inputs, combined with frictions in those markets, poverty traps could still result in theory, as we saw above.

At the same time, we saw that multiple frictions are necessary but not sufficient for poverty traps. Therefore, one has to be very careful in interpreting existing evidence to infer the presence or absence of poverty traps and not conclude from any single piece of evidence for or against the presence of a specific friction that poverty traps at the individual level exist or not (as, e.g., Kraay and McKenzie [2014] seem to do).

Second, if capital is the only input or all other inputs have perfect rental or sales markets so that capital is, in effect, a "sufficient" input (for example, in the presence of cash-in-advance constraints), and so capital market frictions play a central role in determining whether poverty traps could arise. In this case, capital market frictions or restrictions on intertemporal resource allocation are necessary for friction-driven poverty traps to emerge independent of any other frictions. Third, if inputs other than capital are needed for production (such as human capital or land) and these markets are subject to imperfections, then the previous conclusion has to be modified. In such cases, even if (short-term) capital markets are perfect we could get poverty traps. We saw this could happen if the production technology is non convex with respect to it and there are intertemporal borrowing constraints due to either restrictions on negative bequests or frictions in capital markets for long-term loans.

7. A deeper issue is what are the underlying sources of these frictions in capital markets and markets for other inputs, and to what extent they may be interrelated. As we know from the literature of land reform (see Mookherjee 1997) if there are agency problems, a landlord will not sell off his land to his tenant or offer a fixed rent contract instead of a sharecropping contract, even though that will give the tenant better incentives because the tenant will not be able the afford the price at which the landlord will be willing to sell. However, for exactly the same agency problem, a lender cannot step in and offer the tenant a loan to buy off the land, since in the loan repayment process, the same agency problem will raise its head.

Non-Homothetic Preferences

In the previous subsection we assumed preferences are homothetic and focused on external frictions. Now we assume there are no external frictions, and examine the role of how extreme scarcity may cause the poor behave differently from the nonpoor,andwhetherthiscanlead topovertytraps. For example,the poor may discount the future too heavily, be too risk averse, may not care enough about their children, or may be more subject to various behavioral biases. With non-homothetic preferences, income effects can play an important role, and in particular, even though the deep preference parameters are the same (b in our framework) and there are no external frictions, for low levels of income individuals may behave differently (in terms of how much they save or leave as bequests) and this can reinforce low incomes, generating a very different mechanism for a poverty trap. We call these kind of poverty traps scarcity-driven poverty traps.8 While we focus on money, we also discuss the relevant scarce resource being time or attention span.

This argument is to be distinguished from one which says preference-related parameters have an effect on an individual's economic outcome. That is a conditional convergence type argument: for example, those who do not put enough weight on the future (lower b) will end up with a lower steady state income. The main idea is there is no external friction to be potentially fixed to help people get out of a poverty trap. What is interesting about scarcity-driven poverty traps is that, short of a direct transfer of income or a general increase in productivity (an increase in A that raises p , for example) they can persist even when a whole range of supply-side interventions aimed at fixing various kinds of market failures are in place. We avoid calling this class of poverty traps ``behavioral" poverty traps because that may be confused with those arising from behavioral biases only (e.g., loss aversion, hyperbolic discounting, excessive expenditure on temptation goods). That is certainly a possible channel, as we discuss below, but it is possible to have these kinds of poverty traps with standard preferences as well, as the model below indicates. Scarcity Driven Poverty Traps - The Benchmark Model As in the benchmark one-input model of section 2, assume that output is given by $q \frac{1}{4} Af(k)$ where the technology is convex, and that capital markets are perfect, so that the income of an individual is $yt \frac{1}{4} p$ þrkt where $p \frac{1}{4} max k AfðkÞrk$:

8. Azariadis (1996) provided an overlapping generations version of a model that is similar in spirit to the one that is presented in this section. As before, let us assume agents derive utility from consumption c and from bequest b. Even though in a narrow sense b captures financial bequests, we can interpret it as any investment (e.g., human capital) from current income that enhances the productive capacity of children (e.g., health, education). Even though this is the interpretation we will focus on, as earlier, we could also view b as saving or an investment in an individual's own human capital. For now, let us assume b 0 but we will see below that in this particular model, this "friction" that constrains intertemporal resource allocation, does not play a major role. In addition, we allow individuals to consume a luxury good z. The utility function is given by: $Uðc;bÞ \frac{1}{4} logcþ$ b logðbþBÞþ g logðzþZÞ where B . 0, Z . 0,b [ð0;1Þ, and g [ð0;1Þ. We assume that the marginal utility of bequests at $b \frac{1}{4} 0$ is higher than the marginal utility of luxury goods when $z \frac{1}{4} 0$:b B. g Z :We can think of c as basic consumption, b as money passed on to children, and z, a luxury good (durables, a vacation) which is not essential for survival but is consumed as income goes up.

Our assumption will ensure that for low levels of income, all income is spent on c, for moderate levels of income it is split between c and b, and finally, for high levels of income it is split between c, b, and z. Total income at time t is $yt \frac{1}{4} p$ þrkt and as before, $ktþ1 \frac{1}{4} bt$. The budget constraint is ct þbt þzt $\frac{1}{4} p$ þrkt: It is straightforward to derive that there will be two income thresholds, y and y, and two corresponding thresholds for capital: k ; B bp b r and k ;ð1þ b ÞZ g B gp g r such that k . k.

This follows from our assumption b B. g Z Using the fact that bt ¼ ktþ1, we get the dynamics of how the capital stock will evolve: ktþ1 ¼0 for k k ¼ b 1þ b ðrkt þ p Þ B 1þ b for k k k ¼ b 1þ b þ g ðrkt þ p Þð1þ g ÞB b Z 1þ b þ g for kt k: This is depicted in figure 4. We have assumed in the figure that b 1þ b r . 1 . b 1þ b þ g r and B bp . 0 (which is likely in economies with low productivity, namely, a low level of A). Moreover, for a poverty trap to result, the middle segment of the equation of motion needs to intersects the 458 line at a point that is lower than k, the specific condition being B bp b rð1þ b Þ , k.

Under these conditions, families that start poor (capital stock less than k) don't save at all and therefore, have a steady state capital stock of 0, those who start with more than k grow rapidly up to the point where the saving rate falls (as luxury consumption kicks in), and they converge to a high capital stock (k*). Of course, if the above conditions are not satisfied, it is possible to have a unique steady state (e.g., if B bp 0).

As noted above, so far we assumed b 0: Suppose we allow b , 0 (but smaller in absolute value than B, given the utility function we have assumed), that is, parents can borrow against the earnings of their children that the children will have to pay off. Given that in the current framework, this borrowing cannot be used to invest in the human capital of children that will generate returns in the next period, this option turns out not to be consequential. In particular, it is straightforward to show that instead of b¼0, for families starting with low initial levels of assets, b , 0 (as opposed to b¼0) will be a stable steady state under conditions similar to those derived above, in addition to a high wealth steadystate. Time Rather than Money Being the Scarce Resource The sources poverty traps that are possible if preferences are non-homothetic in income, can be more general than in the specific channel developed above. For example, the scarce resource in question may be time or attention span or cognitive capacity rather than physical or financial capital. Suppose individuals can allocate time between generating current income, and spending it with their children to help develop their human capital. Assume income depends on human capital only, and physical or financial capital plays no direct role in production. In particular, suppose the budget constraint is: ct whtðT ltÞ

where ct is consumption, lt is the time spent with children, and ht is human capital at time t. We assume that w is the exogenously given wage rate per unit of human capital, so that someone with twice as much human capital will earn twice as much for the same amount of time spent working. Also, let htþ1 ¼ htlt be the equation of motion of human capital - a more educated parent is more effective in converting her time spent with the children to transmit human capital to them.9 Suppose preferences are similar as before: logct þ b logðlt þBÞþ g logðzþZÞ: It is straightforward to check that, for low levels of ht, individuals may choose l¼0 and we can have a poverty trap. Extending the Scarcity Channel It is possible to extend the scarcity channel to consider how it interacts with insufficient intergenerational altruism, as well as various behavioral biases. Interpreting b broadly as any investment in the productive capacity or welfare of children, suppose society puts a greater weight

9. Notice that, in principle, we can allow for a market in hiring a private tutor - parents can buy h0l units worth of human capital for their children by paying an amount wh0, where h0 can be different from ht. What matters here is full income in the sense of Becker. (say, ^ b) on the welfare of children (or, in the case of gender bias, a greater weight on the welfare of female children) than parents do (i.e., b) where ^ b . b . Given the income effect identified under the scarcity channel, we can readily see that the gap between the socially optimal level of investment and what will be chosen by parents will be larger, the poorer are the parents.

Similarly, we can allow individuals to have behavioral biases in addition to the channel of limited time or attention span discussed in the previous subsection (see, e.g., Banerjee and Mullainathan 2010; Bernheim, Ray, and Yeltekin 2013).

The point is not that only the poor are subject to these kinds of biases, but that low incomes exacerbate these biases, or, their negative consequences. A satisfactory treatment of this issue is beyond the scope of the present exercise but we can modify the benchmark model above to briefly examine the implications. Suppose we introduce an inessential consumption good (e.g., tobacco or alcohol) v and add the term d logðvþVÞ (where d [½0;1 and V . 0) to the utility function and make the assumption d V . b B. This is similar to what Banerjee and Mullainathan (2010) call a temptation good. By a familiar argument, individuals will spend all their income on c for very low levels of k, but now they will spend some of their incomes on v as k crosses a threshold, and only for a higher threshold they will choose a positive value of b. Earlier, a cash transfer to increase the financial resources of a poor family above k would be sufficient to help them escape the poverty trap. But now, there is an intermediate range of k such that an unconditional cash transfer will partly get frittered away on v, an issue we will touch upon in section 4 where we discuss anti-poverty policy. Barro-Becker Altruistic Preferences A reasonable question to ask is, will our results go through if rather than having warm-glow type preferences where parents care about the bequests they pass on to their children, they cared about the utility of their children, and through a recursive argument, all future generations. Even with Barro-Becker altruistic preferences (as introduced in section 3.1), it is possible to get multiple steady states without any external friction. For example, it has been shown that such an outcome may occur when the poor discount the future too heavily (see, e.g., Iwai [1971] and Azariadis [1996] for more references on these kind of "impatience traps"). We can illustrate the basic argument quite simply. Suppose an individual maximizes X 1 t¼0 b t lnðctÞ:

Let kt be capital at time t, let capital markets be perfect with a constant interest rate r.1, and let there being no constraints on intertemporal transfers. For simplicity, suppose individuals earn a constant flow of income yt ¼y every period. Then the per-period budget constraint is: ktþ1 ¼ rðkt þyctÞ: Dynamic optimization yields the standard Euler equation: ctþ1 ct ¼ b r: If b is less than 1 r the individual will run down his assets, with decreasing consumption levels, and will eventually reach a steady-state where he would just consume at the subsistence level (e.g., assuming a constraint like ct c . 0 for all t). If instead b is greater than 1 r then he will accumulate assets, with rising consumption levels over time. If b ¼ 1 r then there would be a steady-state with a constant consumption level (higher than the subsistence level) every period. If the discount factor b is increasing in c and for low levels of c, b , 1 r, we can readily see the possibility of multiple steady-states.

This suggests that our results on strong income effects leading the poor to save too little are not dependent on the particular set of preferences of the individual or the particular form of nonhomotheticity we introduced earlier. Combining Friction and Scarcity Driven Poverty Traps Clearly, external frictions and income effects can coexist and can combine to generate poverty traps. Indeed, Banerjee and Mullainathan (2008) is an example of this.

10 Their core model is similar to the time allocation problem in the previous subsection.11 They juxtapose this with a model where human capital affects income via productivity but there are nonconvexities in this relationship, while current human capital depends in a linear fashion on the previous period's human capital. As we saw in section 3.1, these two features are sufficient to generate poverty traps via the external frictions channel alone. Therefore, from the theoretical point of view, having both these channels is not necessary to generate poverty traps. However, the interaction between scarcity and friction driven poverty traps does raise interesting conceptual issues. For example, in an environment where the population is very poor, there will be little incentives for suppliers of specific inputs to set up shop due to lack of sufficient demand, and so supply-side frictions may be endogenous. We will return to this issue when discussing policy in the next section. Another example of a combination of a friction-driven and a scarcity-driven poverty trap is when individuals are risk-averse and the degree of risk-aversion is decreasing in income (e.g., if the utility function displays decreasing absolute risk aversion). The poor will focus on low risk and low-returns projects, while the rich will focus on high risk and high-returns projects, and these can generate poverty traps. However, this argument implicitly assumes insurance markets being imperfect, because otherwise, with full insurance all individuals would maximize the certainty equivalent of their income and this kind of poverty trap

10. Similarly, Moav (2002) shows that a convex bequest function may lead to poverty traps using a utility function that leads to corner solutions in bequests that are similar to us. However, he assumes capital markets to be imperfect. 11. In their model, individuals

121

either choose all of their time (or attention span) at home or at work, but as we saw above, one can get a poverty trap even with interior solutions.

Will be difficult to sustain. More generally, it is hard to separate the roles of credit and insurance markets, because if individuals are risk-averse then the optimal contract should factor in both liquidity constraints and uninsured risk (as in the standard principal-agent model where the principal is risk neutral and the agent is risk-averse). Therefore, the emphasis on capital market frictions should be broadened to financial markets more generally when agents are risk-averse. Scarcity-Driven Poverty Traps - The Key Implications The key points from our discussion of scarcity-driven poverty traps are as follows. First, poverty traps can exist even without any external friction due to the operation of strong income effects in the behavior of individuals.

This is possible without any behavioral biases, although it is consistent with the attention span of the poor being overloaded with decisions that have to do with day to day struggle for survival, at the detriment of forward-looking planning or expending greater productive effort at work (Mullainathan and Shafir 2013). Second, as the root cause of scarcity-driven poverty is scarcity, the most obvious policy implication is a lump-sum transfer to the poor. Of course, if there are external frictions to fix (say, in capital markets or in health or education) then these can go together, but there are likely to be strong complementarities between these kinds of policies, as we discuss in the next section. Third, to the extent there are grounds for a paternalistic intervention, because the preferences of the individual is different from that of the policymaker (which can be due to behavioral biases or insufficient intergenerational altruism or gender bias), unconditional lump sum transfers may not be the most efficient form of intervention and there may be a case for other policy instruments (e.g., conditional cash transfers).

WHAT THEORY CAN TELL US ABOUT POLICY

We now turn to discussing the implications of our theoretical framework for the design of anti-poverty policy. Various anti-poverty policies can be divided into three broad categories: those that are aimed at enabling the poor greater access to markets, those that are aimed at improving the access of the poor to public services and infrastructure, and those that are explicitly redistributive in nature. Examples of the first include reducing transactions costs in specific markets (e.g., savings, credit, insurance), providing inputs which are not readily available in the market (e.g., training specific skills), improving access to information, and reforming property rights. Examples of the second include various measures to improve accountability and reduce leakage and corruption in the provision of public services like health and education. Examples of the third class of policies involve directly transferring resources to the poor, in cash or in kind.

Cash transfers can be unconditional, or conditional on children attending school and family members receiving preventative health care (e.g., programs such as Progresa, renamed Oportunidades and more recently, Prospera, in Mexico, and Bolsa Familia in Brazil) or in-kind (e.g., food, sanitation, education, health services provided free or at a subsidized rate to the poor). We will refer to the these as UCTs, CCTs, and IKTs. Given the focus of this article, we will ignore delivery or implementation issues that imply an entirely different set of costs and benefits of alternative antipoverty policies. For example, conditional transfers have the advantage that they can screen out the nonpoor and achieve better targeting than unconditional cash transfers). Similarly, we will not discuss situations where externalities are important (e.g., health interventions like deworming or insecticide-treated bednets) that make certain types of conditional transfers preferable to unconditional ones.12 I will also not attempt a review of the extensive empirical literature evaluating the performance of these programs but rather will make a number of conceptual points based on the framework developed in the previous section.13 The first point is other than improving access to capital and savings, or an UCT, any other single intervention is unlikely to get rid of poverty traps.

This follows from our discussion of friction-driven poverty traps where we saw that other than removing whatever constrains the ability of the poor to borrow and save, no single friction is sufficient to trap individuals in poverty. Also, for both friction and scarcity-driven poverty traps, a UCT of an appropriate magnitude will help the poor overcome poverty traps in our framework, unless there are grounds for paternalism, an issue we discuss below. More broadly, this reflects the standard economic argument that unless we know what is the specific friction, it is best to leave it to the recipient to decide what she will do with the savings or loan, or the cash transfer. Only in an extreme case where some critical noncapital input (e.g., training or land) is not available in the market or is very costly, and the income generation technology is non convex with respect to it, there are grounds for intervening directly to make that input accessible to help overcome poverty traps. This is one of the arguments behind the recent policy interest in UCTs. For example, the work of GiveDirectly in Kenya, a charity that gives no-strings attached cash grants, equivalent to almost two year's worth of local income, to the poor has received a lot of attention. While long-term impacts are yet to be known, at least in the short run the impacts are quite good in terms of helping build assets, encouraging investment in, and generating revenue from businesses (Haushofer and Shapiro 2013). In addition, several studies using randomized field experiments have highlighted the importance of capital and access to savings technology. A well-known study by De Mel et al. (2008) have found high potential rates of return to capital in small business among Sri Lankan microenterprise owners that far exceed formal sector interest rates. Another important study shows that providing access to non-interest bearing bank accounts led to significant increase in savings, productive investments and private expenditures (Dupas and Robinson 2013).

12. We refer the reader to Das et al (2005) for a good discussion of some of these issues. 13. See, e.g., Baird et al (2013) for a review of CCTs and UCTs in the context of developing countries.

Second, even with policies that improve access to capital or savings or a UCT, at best poverty traps in a narrow sense will be eliminated. That is, two individuals who, except for income or wealth (y or k in terms of our model), are identical will not end up very differently in the long run. But if other markets are underdeveloped (e.g., acquiring skills), infrastructure is poor, then neither will do very well. In terms of our model the main problem is A is low, that is, the problem of conditional convergence remains and individuals who are otherwise identical but live in better environments (in terms of market access, infrastructure) will do better. As noted above, cash transfers or facilitating borrowing or saving will have limited impact on incomes if markets for certain critical (noncapital) inputs are not developed. In such circumstances, a direct intervention in improving A (or, encouraging migration from a low A to a high A area) may be the best policy, and an excessive focus on poverty traps can distract our attention from this more basic problem.

Indeed, even if there does not exist multiple steady states, the elasticity of response to changes in certain policies can be quite high. In the version of the Solow model we discussed in the previous section, the steady-state level output is q ¼ðAÞ 1 1 a s a 1 a , i.e., the steady state output is a convex function of A and so elasticity of response to policy changes could be quite high. Third, a mix of interventions that relax the budget constraints of the poor and remove certain external frictions are likely to yield significantly high returns compared to an intervention that addresses only one of these problems. For example, if we fix financial markets or give a large cash grant, and improve access to training or infrastructure, gains are likely to be much higher than these individual interventions. Recall from our basic model that q¼Af(k), that is, k and A are complements. If due to external frictions k is lower than what it could be as dictated by the deep parameters, then a direct lump-sum transfer can be used to raise k but suppose that some of these resources could also be spent to increase A. Given the complementarity between k and A, it is likely that rather than spending the available funds either on increasing k or on improving A only, the gains will be larger if it is split between the two. Indeed, Bandiera et al. (2013) find that sizable transfers of assets and training to impart skills in Bangladesh enable the poorest women to shift out of agricultural labor and into running small businesses, which persists and strengthens after assistance is withdrawn, and leads to a 38% increase in earnings. Similarly, Blattman et al. (2014) find that cash transfers coupled with business training are very effective among impoverished Ugandan women. In contrast, McKenzie and Woodruff (2014) review training business owners from a dozen randomized experiments and find little lasting impact on profits or sales.

Fourth, some interventions (e.g., credit, savings) are likely to have similar effects, and it is important to diagnose which underlying friction is more important. For example, if the main problem facing the poor is that they do not have access to a good savings technology (with or without self-commitment problems), then availability of small loans to be paid in short installments via microfinance may help them smooth consumption or purchase durables, but a better

solution yet might be to improve their ability to save. Indeed, Dupas and Robinson (2013) find that the take-up for their savings package is very high (87%), in contrast to the relatively low take-up rate in most rigorous studies of microfinance (e.g., 27% in the study by Banerjee et al. [2014] of a microfinance in India), and this suggests that access to a good saving technology may be a higher priority for the poor. Finally, we turn to the question of under what circumstances CCTs may be strictly preferred to UCTs. In our model this can happen only in the case where the individual's preference and the policymakers preference differs, due to the presence of behavioral biases (e.g., excessive weight on temptation goods or present consumption), insufficient intergenerational altruism, or gender bias.14 As we saw, a low value of b coupled with low incomes can generate poverty traps. Even though there isn't that much evidence that the poor fritter the money away (Evans and Popova 2014), there is fairly compelling evidence that CCTs are more effective than UCTs in raising educational outcomes.

Baird et al. (2013) studied twenty-six CCTs, five UCTs, and four programs that ran both in parallel and found that school enrollment rose by 41% on average across all the CCT programs, while under the UCT programs, the increase was 25%. This does not necessarily mean CCTs are better in welfare terms than UCTs, but as with taxes or subsidies on a specific good or service, it does affect behavior through the standard combination of price and income effects. Also, if the amount the poor invest on children (b in our model) depends on income (y) or wealth (k) in a way that is convex over some region (as in section 3.2), then given the complementarity between A and k noted above, combining a UCT with a policy that directly tackles a friction on the supply side (say, better schools or health facilities) or raises overall productivity A, is likely to yield higher returns than a policy (with a comparable budget) that makes a cash transfer conditional on individuals undertaking a certain minimum investment in b. However, if indeed the underlying grounds for paternalism are strong or externalities are significant, then arguments in favor of CCTs continue to be valid.

CONCLUSION: We developed a conceptual framework to examine conditions under which individuals can be trapped in poverty, distinguishing between the role that external frictions play, versus those that are due to choices made under extreme scarcity. We then applied this framework to discuss various types of anti-poverty policies, distinguishing between policies that are aimed to facilitate market access for the poor, and those that are redistributive in nature, and in the latter category, discussed the relative merits of unconditional and conditional cash transfers and in-kind transfers.

14. As noted earlier, we are ruling out screening issues in targeting the poor, or more generally, implementation-related issues.There are several related and interesting issues that we did not address. First, we worked with a representative agent framework and this precludes many interesting issues that heterogeneity among individuals raise. Even within the same area and similar socioeconomic characteristics, individuals have different preferences, abilities, beliefs, and aspirations; therefore, we have to think beyond a one-size-fits-all policy. Indeed, most studies evaluating specific policies find significant heterogeneity in their impact on different individuals. Second, we did not discuss problems of implementation, including targeting, and this raises a whole new set of interesting issues. Third, the policy interventions that we discussed are likely to alter individual behavior if they are expected to be in place, and as the discussion of various welfare programs in developed countries suggest, it is important to study the incentive effects of various anti-poverty policies, rather than viewing them as being administered from "outside the system" to lift the poor out of poverty. Finally, another interesting issue is how to diagnose what the most binding constraint is in a given environment at the microeconomic level, similar in spirit to the growth diagnostics approach (see Rodrik 2010).

Is it an external friction, and if so, which one (see Karlan et al. [2014] for an interesting experiment along these lines), or is it really the behavior of the poor under extreme scarcity? All these, and undoubtedly many more, seem potentially exciting avenues of future research.

CONNECT WITH THE WIDER WORLD TO UNDERSTAND YOUR WORLD; BE ACTIVE TAKE LONG WALKS, MAKE YOURSELF AWARE OF YOUR INNER SELF, AND TAKE NOTICE OF YOUR SURROUNDINGS IN YOUR LIFE TO IMPROVE YOUR LIFE. KEEP SEARCHING FOR KNOWLEDGE, KEEP LEARNING AND TRYING SOMETHING NEW EACH DAY. TO GET YOU HAVE TO GIVE....By Vincent happy Mnisi

The Freedom Charter puts it plain and Simple!

I suggest that this Charter be adopted by every country in the world, if the world adopts this Charter the world will soon become a world of abundance for all... 'THESE FREEDOMS WE WILL FIGHT FOR, SIDE BY SIDE, THROUGHOUT OUR LIVES, UNTIL WE HAVE WON OUR LIBERTY.' Adopted at the Congress of the People, Kliptown, South Africa, on 26 June 1955. We, the People of South Africa, declare for all our country and the world to know: that South Africa belongs to all who live in it, black and white, and that no government can justly claim authority unless it is based on the will of all the people; that our people have been robbed of their birthright to land, liberty and peace by a form of government founded on injustice and inequality; that our country will never be prosperous or free until all our people live in brotherhood, enjoying equal rights and opportunities; that only a democratic state, based on the will of all the people, can secure to all their birthright without distinction of colour, race, sex or belief; And therefore, we, the people of South Africa, black and white together - equals, countrymen and brothers - adopt this Freedom Charter. And we pledge ourselves to strive together, sparing neither strength nor courage, until the democratic changes here set out have been won.

The People Shall Govern!

Every man and woman shall have the right to vote for and to stand as a candidate for all bodies which make laws; All people shall be entitled to take part in the administration of the country; The rights of the people shall be the same, regardless of race, colour or sex; All bodies of minority rule, advisory boards, councils and authorities shall be replaced by democratic organs of self-government.

All National Groups Shall Have Equal Rights!

There shall be equal status in the bodies of state, in the courts and in the schools for all national groups and races; All people shall have equal right to use their own languages, and to develop their own folk culture and customs; All national groups shall be protected by law against insults to their race and national pride; The preaching and practice of national, race or colour discrimination and contempt shall be a punishable crime; All apartheid laws and practices shall be set aside.

The People Shall Share In The Country's Wealth!

The national wealth of our country, the heritage of all South Africans, shall be restored to the people; The mineral wealth beneath the soil, the banks and monopoly industry shall be transferred to the ownership of the people as a whole; All other industry and trade shall be controlled to assist the well-being of the people; All people shall have equal rights to trade where they choose, to manufacture and to enter all trades, crafts and professions.

The Land Shall Be Shared Among Those Who Work It!

Restrictions of land ownership on a racial basis shall be ended, and all the land redivided amongst those who work it, to banish famine and land hunger; The state shall help the peasants with implements, seed, tractors and dams to save the soil and assist the tillers; Freedom of movement shall be guaranteed to all who work on the land;

All shall have the right to occupy land wherever they choose; People shall not be robbed of their cattle, and forced labour and farm prisons shall be abolished.

All Shall Be Equal Before The Law!

No one shall be imprisoned, deported or restricted without a fair trial; No one shall be condemned by the order of any Government official; The courts shall be representative of all the people; Imprisonment shall be only for serious crimes against the people, and shall aim at re-education, not vengeance; The police force and army shall be open to all on an equal basis and shall be the helpers and protectors of the people; All laws which discriminate on grounds of race, colour or belief shall be repealed.

All Shall Enjoy Equal Human Rights!

The law shall guarantee to all their right to speak, to organise, to meet together, to publish, to preach, to worship and to educate their children; The privacy of the house from police raids shall be protected by law; All shall be free to travel without restriction from countryside to town, from province to province, and from South Africa abroad; Pass Laws, permits and all other laws restricting these freedoms shall be abolished.

There Shall Be Work And Security!

All who work shall be free to form trade unions, to elect their officers and to make wage agreements with their employers; The state shall recognise the right and duty of all to work, and to draw full unemployment benefits; Men and women of all races shall receive equal pay for equal work; There shall be a forty-hour working week, a national minimum wage, paid annual leave, and sick leave for all workers, and maternity leave on full pay for all working mothers; Miners, domestic workers, farm workers and civil servants shall have the same rights as all others who work; Child labour, compound labour, the tot system and contract labour shall be abolished.

The Doors Of Learning And Of Culture Shall Be Opened!

The government shall discover, develop and encourage national talent for the enhancement of our cultural life; All the cultural treasures of mankind shall be open to all, by free exchange of books, ideas and contact with other lands; The aim of education shall be to teach the youth to love their people and their culture, to honour human brotherhood, liberty and peace; Education shall be free, compulsory, universal and equal for all children; Higher education and technical training shall be opened to all by means of state allowances and scholarships awarded on the basis of merit; Adult illiteracy shall be ended by a mass state education plan; Teachers shall have all the rights of other citizens; The colour bar in cultural life, in sport and in education shall be abolished.

There Shall Be Houses, Security And Comfort!

All people shall have the right to live where they choose, to be decently housed, and to bring up their families in comfort and security; Unused housing space to be made available to the people; Rent and prices shall be lowered, food plentiful and no one shall go hungry; A preventive health scheme shall be run by the state; Free medical care and hospitalisation shall be provided for all, with special care for mothers and young children; Slums shall be demolished, and new suburbs built where all have transport, roads, lighting, playing fields, creches and social centres; The aged, the orphans, the disabled and the sick shall be cared for by the state; Rest, leisure and recreation shall be the right of all; Fenced locations and ghettoes shall be abolished, and laws which break up families shall be repealed.

There Shall Be Peace And Friendship!

South Africa shall be a fully independent state, which respects the rights and sovereignty of all nations; South Africa shall strive to maintain world peace and the settlement of all international disputes by negotiation-not war; Peace and friendship amongst all our people shall be secured by upholding the equal rights, opportunities and status of all; The people of the protectorates-Basutoland, Bechuanaland and Swaziland-shall be free to decide for themselves their own future; The right of all the peoples of Africa to independence and self-government shall be recognized and shall be the basis of close

"Limitations are like mirages created by your own mind. When you realise that limitation do not exist, those around you will also feel it and allow you inside their space"...By Stephen Richards

PhD in Philosophy Proposal

"Why and what is keeping all Mankind from living in Abundance?"

University of Sunderland 2020

By

Vincent Happy Mnisi Student No: 199250855

Introduction

The aim of this research will be to discover why Mankind is not living an abundant life, with the current technologies available to mankind. This research will prove that everyone can and should be living an Abundant life. This research will embark upon showing how some cultures have more abundance than others, the how and why different educational cultural upbringings with formal education and community support can play an important role in creating an Abundant life.

This research aims to research how countries such as Switzerland and Norway have managed to achieve post scarcity. This research will embark upon researching Abundant living Families, and communities the aim is to discover how they acquired it? The Research will also focus on families and communities who are not living an Abundant life? The purpose of this research will be to outline the different thinking processes taken over problem solving and the different mentalities from each community when faced with similar problems.

Methodology:

Participative research (PR) is a method where the primary goal is to create an environment and process where context-bound knowledge emerges to develop 'local theory' that is understandable and actionable. PR is initiated by the organization of interest. The researcher and participants collaborate actively in a loosely defined group process to study and change their social reality. (Whyte, 1989)

All members of the organization can participate. Participants must have the will and resources to participate and take on active roles and directly influence defining the problem, choose the methods used to gather the data, analyze the data, prepare the findings, and create action. (Boga, 2004) (Elden, 1981, 258). The wholistic process is group led and self-organized, and adapts to changes as needed. Results are jointly prepared, and reported to those affected. The group decides when the group is finished. Participants treat each other as colleagues. Through the give and take of a dialogic process, the researcher and participants learn together. The researcher's role as one of many 'co-learners' is not as an expert, but as a 'co-producer of learning.' The researcher is dependent on where and how the data comes, has less control over the research design process itself, and has to be flexible to the perspectives and definitions of the participants. The researcher is not merely a bystander but needs to contribute toward the creation and discovery of a process that can stand on its own.

134

A participative researcher needs to develop a context-sensitive framework, be flexible to changes in the framework based on the local knowledge from participants in their own terms, and solve problems. The result of this type of collaboration is very context-oriented to create new shared understandings. (Reason & Rowan, 1981). As Sohng (1995) comments, participatory research is a collaborative and empowering process because it (a) brings isolated people together around common needs and problems; (b) validates their experiences as the foundation for understanding and critical reflection; (c) presents the knowledge and experiences of the researchers as additional resources upon which to critically reflect; and (d) contextualises what might have previously felt like personal, individual problems or weaknesses.

The primary strength of an action-oriented or participatory approach to research is therefore not about description but about trying things out. It is a research approach that sees its function as one of giving us different ways of relating to natural and social environments. Researchers need to be aware of how members of a group perceive and speak about their lives. This means they must endeavour to find out everything that can be found out about the community being researched. The research will also use Observation Research methods of Observation methods. The Research will utilise the internet, using social media with online questionnaires for communities too and families. Opinion based research methods generally involve designing an experiment and collecting quantitative data. (Sohng, 1995)

For this type of research, the measurements are usually arbitrary, following the ordinal or interval type. Quantifying behavior is another way of performing this research, with researchers often applying a 'numerical scale' to the type, or intensity, of behavior. Observational research is a group of different research methods where researchers try to observe a phenomenon without interfering too much. Observational research methods, such as the case study Observational research tends to use nominal or ordinal scales of measurement. (Reason & Rowan, 1981)

Observational research often has no clearly defined research problem and questions may arise during the course of the study. Observation is heavily used in social sciences, behavioral studies and anthropology, as a way of studying a group without affecting their behavior. In an ideal world, experimental research methods would be used for every type of research, fulfilling all of the requirements of falsifiability and generalisation of the answers on the questionnaire on the interviews conducted. Participant and non-participant observation studies which involve observing people can be divided into two main categories, namely participant observation and non-participant observation. The Researcher considered using the Delphi Research Method which has been considered particularly useful in helping researchers determine the range of opinions which exist on a particular subject, in investigating issues of policy or clinical relevance and in trying to come to a consensus on controversial issues. The objectives can be roughly divided into those which aim to measure diversity and those which aim to reach consensus. (Whyte, 1989)

Background of Research

"Mankind's main purpose on earth is to discover self and to become a purpose for humanity" This book 'Abundance' investigates how wealth is a false construct and how everyone can live in abundance but due to the Capitalistic Systems in place which has a world of scarcity when there is actually enough for everyone to live in abundance. "Our planet produces enough food to feed its entire population. Yet, tonight, 854 million women, men and children will be going to sleep on an empty stomach." an Address by Dr Jacques Diouf, the Director-General of the Food and Agriculture Organization of the United Nations (FAO) at the World Food Day Ceremony in Rome on October 16, 2007, and we have England with so much Gold but no gold mine?.(Mnisi,2020)

Many people think they want to accomplish what other successful people have in life. People often see the surface of worldly achievements, but seldom consider that many of those attainments are constructs of a false world, full of traps and endless enticements that lead to nowhere. People tend to believe they want success, and more toys and things, but when they focus on them, to their bewilderment, those very things move out of their reach.(Mnisi, 2020)

The author's version of success is that life should be full, purposeful, beautiful and boundless. The Author attributes this success to his spirituality, his good health, and community of positive relationships which have all come as a creation of choice. Success comes from finding your center and your self; being self-centered in a positive and peaceful way. This reseacrh will investigate how Ecomomic Systems of Control eveloved and what lead to their developments, who and what drove them into practice from Slavery to our current Economic Slave State of Mind and Being.

This research aims to find out who drove them into practice and who benefited from their existence. This current Capilaitics System we have in place has been set by tenants that were established by the Roman Catholic Church in the early 1500's. Money shouldn't be a means to an end and not a need for every human being. Every human should be paid by their Tax Systems which their families contribute to through Tax Levies Systems devised to keep the cash in circulation and to get rid of products from outlets. Money should be made free to Humans as it's a means for eating and living, hence every Human Being deserves to live a life without any strife or want as they should be looked after by their Tax Systems when out of work or even sponsored into their own Business Ventures. People should never be stressed because of Economic Systems. (Mnisi, 2018)

Life should never be about competition but it is fulfilling your earthly purpose of living a life of love, fulfilling your every Human Need and Human Wants without needing to worry about Economics Systems. The Human Being was not born to suffer in the Land of Sunshine, Milk and Honey. Life should not be full of strife, we are all now Economic Slaves now chasing paper money, we are all playing the game monopoly on a real life scale here without the start-up cash to play the game. Capitalism is another Economic Slavery System built to ensure that large Corporations whose foundations can be traced back to Slavery, Colonisation, Imperialism and Neo-Imperialism Systems will continue to own the Worlds Wealth Systemalically which are in the hands and controlled by European run Companies and Establishments. (Mnisi, 2019)

The current world's biggest Corporations; NGO and Governments have been predominantly led by Europeans who have close ties to one or more Secretive Societies Systems. These Secretive Societies Systems John F Kennedy spoke about in his speech in 1964 appoint Company Directors; Managing Directors of Multinational Companies, NGO's and even select who is going to run for Prime Ministership and Presidency in all countries with a Rothschild Reserve Bank.(Mnisi.2018)

This Capitalistic Systematic World we live in now is full of Cheats, Scoundrels, Manipulative Individuals and Companies wanting in on the next big idea. They swamp any latest innovation like bees to honey. They break down products and recreate their own brands in order to create competition which is at times very unwarranted behaviour and causes losses for the innovators. Capitalism is just pure evil thievery cunning European Mentally which is to discover lands that people lived in and claim to invent products/services that were already invented by other Races. One question I have for the Pro-Capitalist System is "Companies are undying entities if they remain profitable right?" "Why create something that will outlive you amassing Hugh Profits and not giving back to the community that is keeping them profitable?"(Mnisi, 2017)

This World is so inverted that the terrorist is made to look like the good guys and the good guys made to look like the terrorists. American twisted propaganda machine at work here towards its people so they can justify wars imagine going to war against Communism and Islam, And why attack Islamic Countries they are just causing the fight. why? is the question I would love to ask all Americans who hate Communism, why? Capitalism is a worse System Of Control!!!.(Mnisi.2019)

Money shouldn't be a thing to have for a decent living, money should be given out for free by all governments as they should make sure that all their citizens are housed, fed and clothed too. Especially with the Automatisation of Industries which is soon to hit the World. I propose that all companies should issue 20% shares to their Workers in their Annual Profits. My argument is that Workers contribute as much as the owners to make sure that the company remains profitable right? and hence should be rewarded profitably accordingly.(Mnisi, 2018)

Work is an Economic Slavery System in disguise and now everybody in the world is out to get themselves as much Worthless Monoply Paper they can get hold off "Money", That has to get paid into a Bank Account and that Money is then used by the Bankers to make more Money from their Money they must deposit into their Banks, this World is a Systematic Bankers Paradise and they are the only ones profiting from everybody that is living today.(Mnisi.2018)

Inflation is another made up Fallacy System. A visit to South Africa in 2015 was shocking to the author to find that they had priced their bread at R10 from the R2 when he had last been there in 2002, The price of growing wheat never changes right? and they are still paying low wages and it's a Mass Produced Product and Distributed in bulk too, then what is the excuse of making such a price? The South African Financial Auditors need to check their books because it seems like they are making 1000% profits from a subsistence product which should be made as cheap as possible. The problem is that all companies in South Africa are pegging their prices with the Pound and what you buy for 1 pound in England it's worth R18 in South Africa which is fraud the financial regulators are sleeping in South Africa.(Mnisi, 2018)

This research has also noted that each commodity as priced in shops now has the petrol price added upon it as though each product travels into the shops alone and not in bulk. One Principle of Business this research will question the Prices Escalation of Demand Theory, and the Scarcity of Goods Theory of Driving Up Prices. All these are man-made Capitalistic Systems of Business which has made Capitalistic European Markets able to hoard products such as Diamonds and Gold which are not rare but plentiful in Africa.(Mnisi, 2018)

All African Commodities are traded and controlled from Europe, The Gold Market, The Diamond Market; Flower Markets; Cocco Market; and all African Minerals are priced in Europe. Africa is not in control of its natural resources in the same manner Europe or Asia does, The Middle East and Asia control theirs, that's for sure. How can African's be born with such riches at the soles of their feet, grow up poor and are always chasing after European Paper Money. The Middle East has set a precedent by Nationalising all their Oil Reserves, Africa should Nationalise all Mineral Resources for the benefit of Africans today and tomorrow.(Mnisi, 2015)

Europeans have used Reverse Psychology Systems of Manipulative Systems into Making Africans Demand their Monopoly Money in exchange for African Raw Minerals. Before granting Independence in each African Country their Resources were purposely sold off to private entities with their UN; IMF and the World Bank offering crippling loans to the New Nationalist against their resources no wonder countries like Zimbabwe and Zambia were crippled when they had arguments with their Reserves Bank owners.(Mnisi, 2019)

This Capitalistic System has allowed Europe to steal and innovate other people's ideas and religious doctrines all in the name of Capitalism. The backbone of Capitalism in its current form was built by the theft of African Slaves by the Freemasons; Colonialism; Imperialism; Neo-Imperialism and now Fake Independences granted to African countries while the Europeans have full control of the Economies of every African state even printing their monies for their Ex-French Colonies and still in charge of all the other Reserve Banking Systems of the World too. (Mnisi, 2017)

The Rothchild family has a stack in every currency that is being printed in Africa and can make or break it in the World Currency Market System as they control the London Currency Exchange where Currencies values are decided. Capitalism when looked at it Socially is an Exploitative Human System. Its general makeup and after some analysis, The author has realised that his education was Systemically Capitalistically Inclined having Studied Advertising and Business and practicing as an Advertising Executive concluded to that Businesses are an Exploitative Set of Systems setup to Exploit Markets because of the Demand for their products they create Demand for through Advertising and Marketing Activities.(Mnisi, 2019)

Capitalism is built on Competition on who is the best in Class, at Sport, Speaking, Cheating etc. Why create a Competitive Social Environment where people have to compete to seem normal, meaning to be better than normal you have to be number one in a specific field of study or overstanding. Everyone is created differently and we all react differently to everything we learn and our perceptions and interpretations will be different for each individual. Hence the author also believes that the current grading systems in schools undermine the overstandings of different interpretations from each individual's perceptions or it lacks to correct it when the subject is misunderstood too.(Mnisi, 2019)

This current wealth gathering Systematic Driven World is only but just an illusion because wealth are earthly things and shall be left behind when we pass on to the next Life System. Human Beings main pursuit on earth should be to Understand Self and to Overstand their Connection with their Creator by finding their own gifts within which will make them Creative Human Beings that we were born to become. Everyone is born with a Spiritual System within learning to connect with it through Meditation and Solitude should be your goal.(Mnisi, 2020)

Imagine a world where you can grow all your own food in a fully automated greenhouse. Your water falls freely from the sky or wells up from the earth and is filtered and cleaned automatically. Any time you want a new device or product, you can find a design online, perhaps customise it, and fabricate it locally or have it delivered using an efficient automated delivery service. And your children have access to the best education ever conceived, for free and you have access to abundant free energy. What need will you have then to engage with the monetary economy? (Post-Scarcity Article by Posted by Captain Capitalism) accessed online 8/03/2020

The way to bring about a global post-scarcity economy is to help add to the commonly-held resources of mankind. Mankind must learn how to grow their own food and given seeds and then show the exact method of growing away for free on the Internet. Contribute to open-source educational materials. Study whatever you're passionate about and think how you can use it to add value. Social change doesn't come by decree from the politicians' halls. It always comes from the bottom up, from the young vibrant minds who see clearly and say, "I can see a better way to do things". Many grass-roots and open-source type projects are making a real difference in the world right now, so join an existing one or you could inspire others and start your own.

The Universal Commons is the store of information freely available to mankind. It is all about information, and information-management is now the key determinant of success in food production and medical care and digital fabrication will make information the only non-trivial ingredient in physical goods. This trend towards information-rich activities is important because sharing information is non zero-sum, meaning that I can give it to you without diminishing my own supply. If information determines the production of other resources, and that information is free along with abundant material and energy, then global abundance should be possible. Advanced digital fabrications and universal access to information are expected to improve by several orders of magnitude over the course of the next few decades, It could provide the resources for bringing a high quality of life to those that are not currently fortunate enough to have the amenities and services of 'developed' nations. Worthy projects that really ought to happen, can happen and in fact this applies just as much to advanced nations where there is still plenty of inequality and missed opportunities. It will not only provide everyone with the basic necessities for a decent life but give maximum opportunity for people and societies to live and prosper how they might like to. (hdr.undp.org) accessed online 7/3/2020

This means different things to different people. For some it enables a life enhanced by advanced technology, able to do new things they have never been able to before, and for others it means almost the exact opposite allowing them to lead a more basic rural life perhaps with small holdings, more in touch with nature and older ways of living. But they can do this without worrying about a bad year in terms of yield from the land or medical care because of the advanced infrastructure in the background that they can call upon if required.

Post-scarcity almost by definition implies 'post-economic' as economics is based on scarcity. (Pritam Chakraborty June 10, 2019 accessed online 6/3/2020). A post-scarcity society means that the basic necessities of living (and plenty more) will be available for everyone who requires it. There may well still be markets for certain items that have purposefully not been made publicly available or are rare, but for many people this will be irrelevant. It will be a choice and not a necessity to enter that market. The important point here is that for the first time the general population will be able to live comfortably without having to owe anyone else their time.(P.Chakraborty, 2019)

People will not have to suffer drudgery and what amounts to wage slavery during the best years of their lives. Unfortunately a large proportion of people today in both white and blue collar jobs would really rather be doing something else than the jobs they are employed to do. They feel perhaps that what they are doing is not directly relevant to their lives or is not particularly interesting and feel they are simply a cog with little control in a larger machine. Currently they have to do it to afford food, shelter and goods. A post-scarcity society enables them to have the time and space to work on things that are important to them, and to learn the skills needed to reach their goals and have room to be more creative. (Wikipedia) Accessed online 7/3/2020

One scarce resource today for people is time. In a post-scarcity culture, not having to spend the best part of the day working for a living also frees people up to spend more time with each other, something that is vital for a proper community. Both for friendship and mentoring the next generation. However some people feel that increasing automation is a threat. A threat to their livelihoods, a threat to humanity's pride even. The reality is that automation is likely to provide in scenarios where people would prefer not to do that job. (Wikipedia) Accessed online 7/3/2020

It leaves people free to be creative and industrious in activities that they want to be part of and allows for greater variety than the average working life offers today. Open design will enable people to be involved in the creation or customisation of the goods they want in a way not seen before and reverses the trend of people simply being passive consumers. Creativity is something that can give huge satisfaction to people but if not fulfilled can cause great frustration and dissatisfaction. It enables an individual to have more control over their environment and life.

In recent decades resource- abundant developing countries have been underperforming in creating an abundant life for their citizens, when compared with resource-deficient developed countries due to the post colonial and current imperial measures in place benefiting Europe and European companies as they have still maintained private ownership of the mineral rights in the name of capitalism i.e De Beers and Anglo American still own mining rights in Africa post Independence. African economies have the biggest potential for rapid growth due to the fact that most of them also have ample cropland to grow their own food and why Africa is still importing food is amazing to me? Africa should use their mineral exports to further enhance their capacity both to invest and to import compared with the non mineral economies.(Mnisi, 2020)

African governments have to Nationalise all mineral mining resources for the benefit of its citizens to consolidate the wealth they are born with. The disappointing points of performances of the resource abundant countries appears to be robust with regard to the differences in the classification of the natural resource endowment as there is no consensus on the measurement of resource abundance. There is controversy among developed countries concerning the contribution of primary commodities from underdeveloped countries in their early stages of development which can generate the foriegn currency necessary to pay for essential imports and also to service their external debts imposed to keep developing countries in bondage. The IMF and the World Bank work to ensure that developing countries are constantly in debt. In addition extensive Inter African trade which will attracts foriegn investment and modern technology, Growth is therefore maximised by ensuring the maintenance of free internal and external markets for goods and by also allocating capital resources to the populations in the free capital resources to the people in free capital markets. This must be made possible from the age of 18 plus. (Mnisi,2018)

The World needs a Social Service System to look after the world's populations from . This view is opposed by the current economic structure. The World should favour the planning and the setting up non-market allocation of resources through a variety of controls and government incentives for prices for domestic and foriegn trade structures. Structural economist Prebisch (1950) argued in his book that long-run decline in the primary export is an inevitable result of the increasing use of synthetics which is shrinking the need for raw materials causing a low elasticity of demand for raw materials inturn.

Also Prebisch also stated that the Oligopolistic markets in the industrial countries meant that productivity increase there were captured in the form of higher income for workers and owners whereas in developing countries productivity gains were passed on to consumers in the turn of lower prices in turn creating a consumer market which Africans have become. Prebisch also projected a downward trend in the terms of trade from primary commodities in relation to manufactured goods imported by the developing countries Prebich urged the reduced dependency on exporting primary commodities in favour of heavy investment in the manufacturing aimed initially at supplying their domestic markets. The current foriegn exchange system needs to be sterilized in order to introduce a One World Digital Currency to be introduced into society to appreciate in demand. The increase of locally produced commodities competing with imported commodities, the domestic products will increase in demand as their prices will be much lower than imported goods. The manufacturing of products versus importing for resource abundant countries with different natural resources endowment is vital for the local community; these enterprises must be set up to be taxable companies too.

In a post scarcity society the society of abundance in which scarcity has been eliminated, envisaged by some socialist thinkers. Counter-arguments suggest that there are always likely to be scarcities, including positional goods, given that world resources are finite. A postindustrial, or postmodern, order might arise where the impetus to continuous accumulation associated with CAPITALISM was replaced by other goals, and it is in this sense that endemic scarcity might then cease. The post-scarcity age is an anticipated period where due to advancing technology, efficient use of natural resources and co-operation there should exist a great abundance of the material items that everyone needs, achieved with a minimal impact to the environment. (Posted by Captain Capitalism at 8:00 PM online access 08/03/2020

Many fictional visions of post scarcity involve as yet undeveloped technologies but the reality is that global material abundance can be produced with current technologies. Food is one example, where there is more than enough produced for everyone on the planet but politics, economics and logistics prevent fair distribution. The bottom line is that in the fundamental resources of this planet there exists many orders of magnitude more energy, raw material and biological resources than humanity requires, it is a matter of developing systems that use and distribute them more efficiently. By employing open collaborative design, digital manufacturing and advanced automation in combination, everything we need should be trivial to fabricate and distribute from the basics like clean water, good quality food, medecine and suitable housing, to increasingly essential material goods such as vehicles, computers and mobile phones all the way up to purely luxury items. Decentralizing production of these things will also allow more equal access to them and sidestep many of the issues involved in distributing them.

Summary

These methods of research could help identify the tools to acquire significant post scarcity that humankind needs but due to the economic framework we have inherited from previous eras this is not possible. This isn't to say what is proposed here *will* happen, but that it *could* happen it is feasible from a physical and technological viewpoint. It is a matter of spreading the knowledge that these things are possible and enough people choosing to work towards it. Post-scarcity is a theoretical economic situation in which most goods can be produced in great abundance with minimal human labor needed, so that they become available to all very cheaply or even freely. Post-scarcity does not mean that scarcity has been eliminated for all goods and services, but that all people can easily have their basic survival needs met along with some significant proportion of their desires for goods and services. Writers on the topic often emphasize that some commodities will remain scarce in a post-scarcity society. (online access 8/03/2020 Posted by Captain Capitalism at 8:00 PM)

Post scarcity society the society of abundance in which scarcity has been eliminated, envisaged by some socialist thinkers. Counter-arguments suggest that there are always likely to be scarcities, including positional goods, given that world resources are finite. A postindustrial, or postmodern, order might arise where the impetus to continuous accumulation associated with CAPITALISM was replaced by other human goals as stated above. This current CoronaVirus has brought about self isolations and workers who are able to work from home are being encouraged to do so. My personal opinion on this virus is that it's man-made to eradicate human populations worldwide as AI is now ready to take over human labour.

"Limitations are like mirages created by your own mind. When you realise that limitation do not exist, those around you will also feel it and allow you inside their space"...By Stephen Richards

The fact that De Beers still owns the rights to Diamonds worldwide and Anglo American still owns mining rights to African Gold post African-Independence makes one think...By Vincent Happy Mnisi

Bibliography

Abundance *The Future Is Better Than You Think* (Peter H. Diamandis, Steven Kotler, 2014)

(Boga, 2004) *New Economy shift for African Programme* IGI Global, Ltd

Buckminster (Bucky) Fuller quoted on p. XVII in the book <u>Buckminster Fuller Anthology for the New Millenium</u>.

*(*Byrne R, 2006*) The Secret* ATRIA BOOKS New York

(Chase S, 1934) *The Economy of Abundance* Unknown publisher

(Elden, 1981, 258). *Participatory action research and social change* Cornell University

<u>*https://captaincapitalism.blogspot.com/2013/11/why-post-scarcity-economics-is-scary.html*</u>

Page 13 of the United Nation's <u>Human Development Report 2006, Beyond Scarcity: Power, Poverty and the Global Water Crisis at</u> http://hdr.undp.org/en/media/hdr06-complete.pdf
"The world has the technology, the finance and the human capacity to remove the blight of water insecurity from millions of lives".

Page 28 of the United Nation's <u>Human Development Report 2006, Beyond Scarcity: Power, Poverty and the Global Water Crisis at</u> http://hdr.undp.org/en/media/hdr06-complete.pdf

"Of course, water consumption in rich countries does not diminish water availability in poor countries.   Global consumption is not a zero-sum game in which one country gets less if another gets more."

Page 35 of the Human Development Report 2006,Beyond Scarcity: Power, Poverty and the Global Water Crisis at http://hdr.undp.org/en/media/hdr06-complete.pdf

"Globally, there is more than enough water for domestic purposes, for agriculture, and for industry."

The   Guardian

https://www.theguardian.com/books/2013/sep/07/scarcity-sendhil-mullainathan-shafir-review

THE WORLD BANK ECONOMIC REVIEW, Published by Oxford University Press on behalf of the International Bank for Reconstruction and Development / THE WORLD BANK. The World Bank Economic Review Advance Access published April 16, 2015

http://documents.worldbank.org/curated/en/765411468159910121/pdf/805220PUB0WBEc00Box379806B00PUBLIC0.pdfhttp://documents.worldbank.org/curated/en/765411468159910121/pdf/805220PUB0WBEc00Box379806B00PUBLIC0.pdf

P. 123 of World Bank's 2007 World Development Indicators report athttp://tinyurl.com/2epton

 "At the start of the 21st century we have the finance, technology and capacity to consign the water and sanitation crisis to history just as surely as today's rich counties did a century ago."

Page VI in Foreword of the Human Development Report 2006, Beyond Scarcity: Power,   Poverty   and   the   Global   Water   Crisis   at http://hdr.undp.org/en/media/hdr06-complete.pdf

"There is more than enough water in the world for domestic purposes, for agriculture and for industry. The problem is that some people – notably the poor – are systematically excluded from access by their poverty, by their limited legal rights or by public policies that limit access to the infrastructures that provide water for life and for livelihoods."

Page 3 of the <u>Human Development Report 2006,Beyond Scarcity: Power, Poverty and the Global Water Crisis</u> at http://hdr.undp.org/en/media/hdr06-complete.pdf

"Our planet produces enough food to feed its entire population. Yet, tonight, 854 million women, men and children will be going to sleep on an empty stomach."

Address by Dr Jacques Diouf, the Director-General of the Food and Agriculture Organization of the United Nations (FAO) at the World Food Day Ceremony in Rome on October 16, 2007, at http://tinyurl.com/3yfszk on page 2.

"In a world richer than ever before, it is unacceptable that people can be left to die of starvation."

Copied from the report of the United Nations' Special Rapporteur on the Right to Food, Jean Ziegler, March 16, 2006, page 8 at: http://tinyurl.com/38rdgz

From the Foreword of the <u>State of Food Insecurity in the World – 2002</u>, Report of the Food and Agriculture Organization of the United Nations athttp://tinyurl.com/2f667h .

Dosman E *The Global Political Economy of Raul Prebisch* Mcgill University Press 2008
Linkedin: Article by Jacques Poulsen May 23rd 2017 Titled "Digital marketing in an African Context; "will businesses in Africa finally act on the opportunity or remain passive to the dawn of the digital era"?
"https://www.markedu.com/2017/05/23/digital-marketing-africa/

Mckinsey 2018 Report on African digital consumer market https://www.mckinsey.com/industries/financial-services/our-insights/sub-saharan-africa-

Pritam Chakraborty June 10, 2019 accessed online 6/3/2020). *A post-scarcity society means that the basic necessities of living* Article

Masley D,(2017)*Running towards a Post-Scarcity economy* Nest Egg ltd

Mnisi V.H (2018) *The African Black Book.* Manchester: Amazon.uk

Mnisi V.H (2019) *8 Systems.* Sunderland: Amazon.uk

Mnisi V.H (2017) *Life!* Manchester: Amazon.uk

Murray Bookchin, (2004) **Post-Scarcity Anarchism** AK Press Ltd

(Reason & Rowan, 1981). **Human Inquiry,** John Wiley and Sons Ltd

Sadler. P (2012) **Sustainable Growth in a Post-Scarcity World** Gower Publishing, Ltd.

Sohng (1995) *Blending Qualitative and Quantitative Research Methods* Corwin Press Ltd

(Whyte, 1989) *Social Research Methods:* Qualitative and Quantitative Approaches SAGE Publications

Page 3 at http://tinyurl.com/2kvr6v

Page 13 of the United Nation's <u>Human Development Report 2006, Beyond Scarcity:</u> <u>Power,   Poverty   and   the   Global   Water   Crisis   at</u> http://hdr.undp.org/en/media/hdr06-complete.pdf

"The world has the technology, the finance and the human capacity to remove the blight of water insecurity from millions of lives".

-Page 28 of the United Nation's <u>Human Development Report 2006, Beyond</u> <u>Scarcity: Power,   Poverty   and   the   Global   Water   Crisis   at</u> http://hdr.undp.org/en/media/hdr06-complete.pdf

"Of course, water consumption in rich countries does not diminish water availability in poor countries. Global consumption is not a zero-sum game in which one country gets less if another gets more."

-Page 35 of the <u>Human Development Report 2006,Beyond Scarcity: Power, Poverty</u> <u>and the Global Water Crisis at</u> http://hdr.undp.org/en/media/hdr06-complete.pdf

"Globally, there is more than enough water for domestic purposes, for agriculture, and for industry."

–P. 123 of World Bank's 2007 World Development Indicators report athttp://tinyurl.com/2epton *"At the start of the 21st century we have the finance, technology and capacity to consign the water and sanitation crisis to history just as surely as today's rich counties did a century ago."*

The World Bank Economic Review Advance Access published April 16, 2015
Theories of Poverty Traps and Anti-Poverty Policies Maitreesh Ghatak
<u>http://personal.lse.ac.uk/GHATAK/WBERPovTrap.pdf</u>

-Page VI in Foreword of the <u>Human Development Report 2006, Beyond Scarcity:</u> <u>Power,   Poverty   and   the   Global   Water   Crisis   at</u> http://hdr.undp.org/en/media/hdr06-complete.pdf

"There is more than enough water in the world for domestic purposes, for agriculture and for industry. The problem is that some people – notably the poor – are systematically excluded from access by their poverty, by their limited legal rights or by public policies that limit access to the infrastructures that provide water for life and for livelihoods."

-Page 3 of the <u>Human Development Report 2006,Beyond Scarcity: Power, Poverty</u> <u>and the Global Water Crisis</u> at http://hdr.undp.org/en/media/hdr06-complete.pdf

"Our planet produces enough food to feed its entire population. Yet, tonight, 854 million women, men and children will be going to sleep on an empty stomach."

-Address by Dr Jacques Diouf, the Director-General of the Food and Agriculture Organization of the United Nations (FAO) at the World Food Day Ceremony in Rome on October 16, 2007, at http://tinyurl.com/3yfszk on page 2.

"In a world richer than ever before, it is unacceptable that people can be left to die of starvation."

-Copied from the report of the United Nations' Special Rapporteur on the Right to Food, Jean Ziegler, March 16, 2006, page 8 at: http://tinyurl.com/38rdgz

-From the Foreword of the <u>State of Food Insecurity in the World – 2002</u>, Report of the Food and Agriculture Organization of the United Nations athttp://tinyurl.com/2f667h .

Page   11   athttp://tinyurl.com/2kvr6v   and   http://tinyurl.com/ytysvr andhttp://tinyurl.com/ysdtth

https://eduquarks.com/post-scarcity-society-economy/

http://adciv.org/Post-scarcity

https://docs.google.com/document/d/1Uyyx3q5xEVeNaHe5e8LYlzaxDmJYa3 rQwXbw-AzxMvQ/edit#

https://cifs.dk/topics/education/education-in-a-post-scarcity-society/

http://www.unrisd.org/80256B3C005BCCF9/(httpPublications)/D04C41AAF1 FA94FF80256B67005B67B8

https://www.reddit.com/r/PostScarcity/comments/f5q3ka/debate_relating_t o_postscarcity/

https://captaincapitalism.blogspot.com/2013/11/why-post-scarcity-economi cs-is-scary.html

https://simplicable.com/new/post-scarcity

http://adciv.org/Post-scarcity

https://www.quora.com/How-close-are-we-to-a-post-scarcity-society

https://technocracy.fandom.com/wiki/Post_scarcity

https://io9.gizmodo.com/post-scarcity-societies-that-still-have-scarcity-164 0882232

https://en.wikipedia.org/wiki/Post-scarcity_economy

https://www.theguardian.com/books/2013/sep/07/scarcity-sendhil-mullainat han-shafir-review

http://tinyurl.com/2eyl69

http://tinyurl.com/2yjdjv

http://www.usps.com/communications/news/stamps/2004/sr04_043.htm

Page 3 at http://tinyurl.com/2kvr6v

Printed in Great Britain
by Amazon